The Treasure Hunter

The life of the author of *Kidnapped, Treasure Island, A Child's Garden of Verses* and other stories was as romantic and full of adventure as his books. Born in the city of Edinburgh, the son of a lighthouse builder, Stevenson grew to know every nook and cranny of the wild, rocky coast of Scotland. Wherever he went he made friends quickly with unusual people—sailors, shepherds, innkeepers and vagabonds. All of his life he traveled the world over in search of health and adventure: France, England, Italy, California, the South Seas. His observations during these thrilling voyages all found their way into his books which are loved by readers of every age.

Books by Isabel Proudfit

The TREASURE HUNTER

The Story of Robert Louis Stevenson

By ISABEL PROUDFIT

NEW YORK
JULIAN MESSNER

PUBLISHED SIMULTANEOUSLY IN THE UNITED STATES AND CANADA BY
JULIAN MESSNER, A DIVISION OF SIMON & SCHUSTER, INC.,
1 WEST 39 STREET, NEW YORK, N.Y. 10018. ALL RIGHTS RESERVED.

Eighteenth Printing, 1966

Printed in the United States of America

1706
92
STE

1706

Contents

A Boy at Home

Chapter I

What are you able to build with your blocks?
Castles and palaces, temples and docks.
Rain may keep raining, and others go roam,
But I can be happy and building at home.

IT WAS SEPTEMBER in the cold, rainy city of Edinburgh
far away in Scotland. Outside the streets were gray with
fog. Indoors in a room at the top of the house a small
boy lay on the floor before an open fire, building with a
set of wooden blocks.

The boy was building a city—a city beside the sea.
Here the church, there the stores and houses. In the
center, a great palace for the king. From the palace a
flight of steps ran down to the harbor. Going up and
down these steps were several visiting kings, bringing
presents.

The boy himself wore a crown on his head, made of
paper, but the rest of his clothes were more practical.
A green woolen smock, belted at the waist; a small

gray shawl pinned around his shoulders. Beside him on the floor lay a large white handkerchief.

A woman who was in the room with him spoke emphatically:

"Gravy, laddie," she said. "Can ye no leave your building long enough to blow your wee nose? It's plain daft ye are when ye get to making a city."

"Ay, Cummy, ay," said the boy, applying the handkerchief hastily. "But it will soon be tea-time, and the tower is not yet finished."

"Weel, then ye maun finish it after," said Cummy firmly. "Your mither will be up any minute."

"Ay, Cummy, ay," he said, looking at the tower regretfully. "If Mamma is coming up soon, I maun set out the tea-things."

This boy, whom his nurse, "Cummy" or Alison Cunningham, called laddie, was christened Robert Lewis Balfour Stevenson. Later he became known to everyone as Robert Louis Stevenson. In his nursery at home, however, in the rainy city of Edinburgh, in the year 1854, he was called Smout, or Smoutie, more rarely Master Lou. The Smout came from smolt, meaning young salmon or "small fry." This was his father's favorite name for him. Cummy, of course, more often called him Master Lou. As a man grown, his friends called him Louis Stevenson.

Getting up from the floor the boy began to set out the tea-things. A gold crown for his mother, a toasting fork,

4

plates and cups and saucers. The kettle was already boiling on the hearth. Cummy went down to the kitchen for the milk and butter and scones. Usually she brought up an egg for him, too; he liked eggs especially.

When the little gray shawl got in his way, Smout looked down at it sadly. Whenever he had a cold, which was more often than might be expected, Cummy always made him wear the gray shawl.

"It looks so daft wi' my gold crown," he said, twisting it around behind him. . . . "I know . . . let's pretend it is a mantle. Kings always wear a fine velvet mantle, don't they? When Mamma comes up, do you think she will ken why I am wearing it?"

"Ay, laddie, ay," said Cummy, smoothing out his smock where it was rumpled. "And if she dinna ken, ye can tell her."

In a few minutes Smout's mother came up to the nursery. She was a tall, pretty woman with fair hair and blue eyes, quite young to have a son at all, lively and gay with him always. In the daytime at home she wore a soft woolen dress; tonight, however, since she was going out, she wore a rich black silk with an embroidered collar. In this dress, as indeed in every other, Smout thought her the prettiest woman in the world.

Once his mother was there, he lost no time in beginning his "tea," or supper. First they toasted the oatmeal scones over the fire, then spread them with butter and currant jelly. Cummy gave him his egg, which he ate directly from the shell with a small bone spoon. Both his mother and he drank tea, although his had a good deal of milk in it. At the end there was some yellow cake, which Smout jumped up so hurriedly to pass that his paper crown slipped over sideways.

Before they had quite finished, the door opened and a tall man in a frock coat came into the room. This tall man was Smout's father, Mr. Thomas Stevenson. Mr. Stevenson always entered a room like a strong sea-breeze, whether he came from his office or from the lighthouse-ships on which he lived and worked a good deal of the time.

"Now, then, laddie," he said in his man's voice, laying his cold cheek against the boy's face, "What's all this crowning and crowing for? Ye won't be a king when ye grow up, ye'll be a lighthouse-builder like your father and grandfather."

"Nae," said Smout in his small voice, "Nae, Papa, I shall be a soldier."

His father looked at the frail boy with his hair growing in brown curls almost down to his shoulders.

"A soldier is it!" he said, laughing. "Nae, laddie, ye'll be a lighthouse-builder like your father, and lucky to be man enough for that."

After his father and mother had gone, Cummy, whose cheeks were always red, shook out her long, full skirts and brought her work-box to the table. This work-box was made of wood, with gold feet; it was one of Cummy's dearest possessions. The firelight shone on the gold feet and on an enormous cupboard behind it. This cupboard, Cummy had told him, was made by a very wicked man—a man who went to church on Sunday and made fine furniture on weekdays, but became a burglar at night. His name, Cummy said, was Deacon Brody.

Smout, however, knew all about Deacon Brody. What he wanted now was a new story—one that he could act out later. Since most of Cummy's stories came from the Bible, she considered what would please him. The story of Daniel in the Lion's Den, Jonah and the Whale, and a dozen others, he already knew. How about Noah and the great Flood? Yes, that was the one he wanted. While the rain beat on the window outside, and the fire crackled in the grate, she told him of the rain which covered up everything, until the skies were empty and the morning came when the dove did not return to the ark.

Chapter II

When to go out, my nurse doth wrap
Me in my comforter and cap;
The cold wind burns my face, and blows
Its frosty pepper up my nose.

EVERY DAY WHEN the weather was fair Smout went out
to walk with Cummy in the streets of Edinburgh. There
was much to see in these walks. Little black Scottie dogs
with hairy faces, running around cheerfully. Soldiers in
bright uniforms. Above all the city itself rising majes-
tically around him.

Edinburgh is a city built of gray stone on a series of
hills. Rough weather beats upon it a good deal of th
time. The smoke of the chimneys streaks across the sk
From where Smout lived, in a low-lying street to
north of the business district, he could see most of
city.

The street itself was called Inverleith Terrace. At
end of it there were open fields; at the other a small b

river, called the Water of Leith, with buildings on either side of it. Crossing the river by a wooden bridge, and climbing sharply uphill, one came to more stone houses in rows, then the shops and offices where Papa went each day to buy food for the family and do his daily work.

In the very heart of the city, far above Smout at Inverleith Terrace, rose a long narrow hill, with a stone castle built on the very top of it. The people of Edinburgh still call this hill Castle Rock. The castle, Smout learned, was no longer the home of Scottish kings and queens, as it had once been, but was used as a garrison by the soldiers who guarded the city day and night. Every morning and every evening the sound of fifes and drums came from the castle where they were changing the guard. At one o'clock midday, too, a great gun boomed out from the castle. Wherever Papa was at one o'clock, he always pulled out his watch and looked at it to see if it was keeping time correctly.

When the weather was bad, the sky behind Castle Rock was green and murky. On better days, however, the sun touched everything with gold.

Holding Cummy's hand carefully, for he was at that time not quite four years old, Smout walked up and down the streets or into the shops where Cummy bought her thread or wool for knitting. The people in the streets and in the shops talked as Cummy did, using the rich Scottish words Smout loved. They said "faither" for

9

father, "greet" for cry, "dinna" for do not, "maun" for must, "muckle" for much, "claes" for clothes. A small boy was a "wean" or "laddie." Everything small was called "wee" instead of little.

At home Mamma and Papa used some Scottish words, too, but not nearly as many as Cummy. The preacher in church on Sunday was careful to use none at all.

That winter the snow, or "snaw" as Cummy called it, came early.

"Noo," she said, looking out one morning at the first sprinkle, "the winter will soon come fairly."

The snow rarely came to Edinburgh in a thick blanket, any more than the rain fell heavily and steadily in the springtime as it does in other countries. Like every other kind of weather, it came in flurries and patches. But the days were dark and wet, and increasingly cold. When he went out now, Smout wore a woolen muffler tied up tightly around his throat, and stuffed his hands into his pockets.

One morning while he was eating his breakfast by the nursery fire, Cummy discovered a robin pecking stoutly at the window.

"Look noo!" she cried in excitement. "A wee bird out in the crool waither, with nowt (nothing) to eat."

"Shall we give him a bit parritch?" asked Smout, looking down at his oatmeal.

10

"Nae, laddie, crumbs would be best. A bit bannock, and he will be merry again."

She opened the window and scattered crumbs for the robin. After that he came every morning for his breakfast.

The days became shorter, and it was still dark when Cummy lifted Smout out of his bed in the morning. This puzzled him.

"Why, Cummy?" he asked, "Why do we get up in the nicht (night) now?"

"It is no' nicht, laddie, but morning."

"But I see stars shining outside the window."

"Ay, laddie, but still it is morning. In the winter the days are much shorter than they are in summer."

"And in summer," he said, sitting thoughtfully on the edge of the bed, "they are so long that I have to go to bed in the daytime."

"Ay, laddie, but noo ye maun get into your claes. Ye are shivering and shaking."

Smout hurried into his woolen smock, for he did not wear trousers and a jacket. In Scotland in those days boys were not "breeched," as they called it, that is, put into trousers, until they were four or five years old. After that they wore trousers for everyday, pleated plaid kilts on Sundays and holidays. The soldiers up at the castle wore kilts always.

11

As he buttoned up the green smock, Smout hoped that Cummy would not pin the gray shawl over his shoulders. But she did, giving him a gentle pat as she did so. In spite of all the care Cummy gave him, he still took cold more easily than he should have.

Since he must stay in the house most of the day now, Smout played more and more with his blocks. He also played a great deal with toy soldiers, for on his birthday in November he had received a handsome box of soldiers. There were foot soldiers in the new box in red coats and plaid kilts, cavalrymen in white breeches and leather belts, artillery men in brown overcoats. There was even a small cannon from which he could shoot a pea across the room.

Smout built a fort with blocks, or "bricks" as he often called them, in order to fight a real battle. He was the more interested this year, because his own country, Scotland, was at war with Russia in the Black Sea. All that winter and the next English and Scottish armies laid seige to the city of Sebastopol far away in the Crimea.

Smout asked his father and mother many questions about the war. What did the soldiers eat? Where did they sleep at night? Who tied up their wounds when they were hurt in battle? At night when he said his prayers he prayed for the brave soldiers at Sebastopol.

For Christmas that December he received a toy sword. Wishing to tease him, his father said when he saw it,

12

"That is not much of a sword, is it?"

"Oh, yes, Papa," he answered. "It is a silver sword in a gold sheath."

After that he fought a war of his own in the nursery, pretending that chairs were the wicked Russians whom he must cut down with his sword. More and more he was distressed by having to wear the woolen shawl around his shoulders.

"How will people know that I am a soldier?" he asked Cummy anxiously. . . . "I know. I will pretend that I am on a night-march, and this is my blanket. Soldiers *do* carry blankets, don't they?"

"Ay, laddie, ay," said Cummy, and stooped to kiss him, but he brushed her aside. He wanted to forget that he was a boy in a nursery with long brown curls almost down to his shoulders.

A few weeks later Cummy went home to her own village on a visit, which gave Smout's father a chance to do something he had long wanted to do. The curls on the boy's head had worried him; he thought they should be cut off. Sending out for a barber, he stood by while the curls were snipped off and laid in Cummy's workbox with the gold feet. When Cummy came home it would be too late for her to protest that Smout should keep them.

Smout himself, of course, was much pleased with his new appearance. With the curls gone and the Christmas

13

sword buckled to his side, he felt much more a real soldier. The next step would be to persuade everyone to call him Lou instead of Smout or Smoutie. When that was done, he could feel that his baby days were over forever.

"Sneck the door, Mamma," he said, meaning for her to lock it. "I've a story to tell. You write it down."

The story was about himself as a great soldier.

Chapter III

When I was down beside the sea,
A wooden spade they gave to me
To dig the sandy shore.

WHEN WINTER WAS over and summer had come to stay, Smout, or Lou as he was now usually called, went to the seashore for several weeks with his father and mother. The sea was not far away: one could drive easily to it by following the small, brown river at the foot of Inverleith Terrace where he lived. That summer of 1855 the Stevenson family spent the whole month of August at the little seaside village of Portobello not far from Edinburgh.

Lou liked the seashore, because he could dig in the sand all day, or bathe in the pools of seawater along the shore, or ride a donkey up and down at the edge of the water. At night, too, from his bedroom window, he could see the lighthouses twinkle out up and down the coast.

The lighthouses were nice in themselves, and nicer still because he knew that his father had built so many of them. All the men in his father's family seemed to be lighthouse-builders—his Uncle David, his Uncle Alan, and his grandfather, Robert Stevenson. Apparently there was no end to the number of lighthouses needed around the rocky coast of Scotland. Between them his father, Thomas Stevenson, and his Uncle David, who was his father's partner, built twenty-seven shore-lights, twenty-five beacons, and two deep-sea lights during the years they were in business together.

In the spring and fall of each year Lou's father was away from home a great deal looking after this work. Every autumn, too, he took a trip in a special lighthouse-ship to many lighthouses along the coast. During the winter, when he was at home, he spent the business hours of each day planning new harbor-lights or experimenting with new kinds of lamps. No wonder his father was grave and stern at times, Lou thought, with such important work to do.

Lou loved his father dearly, but he was a little afraid of him, too. Papa was not as gentle and patient as Mamma or Cummy. If Lou were naughty, he spanked him. When Lou wanted to tell stories, Papa was not always ready to listen to them.

One day Lou came home from a walk with a stone in his hand. The stone was gray with specks of yellow in it.

'That is gold in my stone," he said to his father, pointing to the specks of yellow. "I will dig them out, and make us all rich."

"Nae, laddie, it is quartz or mica in the gray sandstone. The city of Edinburgh is built on sandstone. The hills of the city, however, like Castle Rock or Calton Hill, are of different rock pushed up through the gray sandstone by volcanic eruption. Some day you will learn all about rocks and their formation."

Lou was not happy over this answer. Some of the big words he did not understand. In any case, the idea of studying rock formation was not as interesting to him as to pretend that there was gold in the gray sandstone. Feeling a little troubled, he went out to find Marion Rhind, his playmate for the summer.

Marion was quite ready to pretend that the stone was full of gold which would make him rich some day. As they splashed happily in a pool of seawater among the rocks, they told each other that they would be married when they grew up, and live in a house by the sea— where there would always be gold in the gray stones.

That night, before he went to sleep, Cummy read Lou the story of Robinson Crusoe on the desert island. While she was reading, his mother came in and sat down beside him. In the middle of the story she asked a question:

"What would *you* do, laddie, if you were cast away on a desert island?"

"I would come away."

"And if the water were all around you?"

"I would come away in a boat."

"And if there were no boat?"

"I would send a letter by the post."

"And if," continued Mamma, "there were no post?"

Lou was at the end of his rope. "Then," he said emphatically, "I would sit down and have a hearty greet (meaning to cry)."

When Mamma laughed, he knew that she had merely been teasing him. But her questions made him uneasy. Somehow down here by the sea the world seemed larger than it was at home, not so safe, harder to manage. In the face of its great vastness he felt small and insignificant.

"Read, Cummy, read!" he said. "I want to hear how Robinson Crusoe got away from the island."

"Ay, laddie, but that took a long time. He had many adventures first."

"But he did get away in the end, did he no', Cummy?"

"Ay, laddie, ay. In the end he got away safely home."

Chapter IV

The child that is not clean and neat,
With lots of toys and things to eat,
He is a naughty child, I'm sure—
Or else his dear papa is poor.

DURING THE WINTER that followed Lou was allowed to
sit up for dinner sometimes with his parents. At first he
had only Sunday dinner with them, an early meal eaten
at five o'clock in the afternoon. Later he was permitted
to eat some weekday dinners with them, too, at six
o'clock. Before this winter he had taken all his meals in
the nursery with Cummy, by the open coal fire.

When his father was home, these dinners were formal
and not quite so merry. When his father was away, however, and he and his mother were alone, they chattered
like two magpies, Cummy said. On these nights one of
their favorite dishes was rabbit-pie. What a treat this
was! The mysterious crust, the steaming meat beneath it,
the potatoes swimming in brown gravy, the whole fla-

19

vored with onion. How much better this was than the weak tea and butterbakes he would have had upstairs. Before he tasted rabbit-pie he had thought the butterbakes delicious—thick, buttery crackers broken up in tea or hot milk. But now he knew that rabbit-pie downstairs with Mamma was better.

How her blue eyes twinkled when he dug into the potatoes; how her fair hair shone in the lamplight. Struggling to cut his meat with a knife that was still too big for him, he often thought, as he had thought before, that she was the prettiest woman in the world. And indeed Mrs. Stevenson was a pretty woman with her fair hair and graceful movements. All her life people admired her.

When the pie was nearly gone, Lou had a sudden thought:

"Other weans over the city," he asked, "are they eating rabbit-pie now, too?"

"Some of them are, laddie, but not all of them. Over behind the castle in the poorer section of the city there are many cold and hungry children. You will walk there some day and see them."

"But the soldiers up at the castle? Do they no' come down and feed them?"

"The soldiers are busy with their duties. Nor do they have food for the hungry children."

"But the weans' mothers and nurses? Why do they no' feed and warm them?"

"Some of the mothers are very poor. They cannot buy food and shelter. Their lives are very bitter."

"Oh, *Mamma*," said Lou. "We should be very *thankful,* shouldn't we, that we have this good dinner before us?"

"Ay, laddie. And all the other things we have, too. Warm clothes and a good home. Books to read and toys to play with. There is your paintbox now waiting upstairs for you."

"Oh, and Mamma, I forgot to tell you. Today I mixed red and blue paint together. It makes the most *beautiful* purple! I painted everything that color."

"Purple is the color for kings," said Mamma. "Everyday people don't often use it."

"Well, if *I* were a king," said Lou, "I would give everyone a warm purple cloak and rabbit-pie for dinner!"

"Bless me, laddie," said Mamma. "What a fine sight the town would be. But now get along upstairs wi' you. Cummy will be waiting."

"Yes, Mamma," said Lou, "But tomorrow I shall paint everyone in my book eating rabbit-pie for dinner."

21

Chapter V

We built a ship upon the stairs,
All made of the back-bedroom chairs.
And filled it full of sofa pillows
To go a-sailing on the billows.

THE FOLLOWING OCTOBER, when Lou was not quite six years old, his cousin, Bob Stevenson, came to spend the winter with him. How exciting that was—how much more fun two boys could have than one. Bob was three years older than Lou—almost nine—and full of grand ideas for fun.

In the morning they played a game with their oatmeal. Bob ate his with sugar but no cream. As he sprinkled the white sugar over the oatmeal he said that it was a country being gradually buried in snow. Lou, on the other hand, ate his oatmeal with hot milk but no sugar. Pouring the milk over the hot cereal, he said that it was a country being gradually submerged by flood. When the oatmeal was entirely covered, the two boys ate up their two countries at breakneck speed.

During the day the boys played more games. Sometimes they dressed up as pirates, soldiers or sailors with
fierce black moustachios made of burnt cork. Once they
built a boat on the stairs, made of chairs from Cummy's
bedroom. In this boat they took various supplies. Lou
said that they must take pieces of bread and a bag of
sugarplums. Bob said that a pail of water and a hammer
and nails would be more useful. In the end they took
the water and the hammer and the nails and an apple
and a slice of cake.

Bob, however, fell out of the boat and hurt his knee,
so that Cummy made them stop playing that game.

For hours together the two boys lay on their stom-
achs on the floor playing a game called "Islands."
Each boy was chief of an important island. Bob's island
was called "Encyclopaedia," Lou's "Nosingtonia." Many
hair-raising adventures happened on these islands—other
islanders attacked them, ships were wrecked on their
shores, monsters swam out of the sea and captured beautiful ladies from the land. So much happened on the
islands, the boys finally wrote histories of them, illustrating the histories with painted pictures. Both Lou and
Bob loved to paint pictures. In fact, Bob grew up to be
an artist, while Lou all his life enjoyed making pictures.

In November Uncle David offered a prize of one
pound (about five dollars in American money) for the
best history of Moses to be written by one of his nieces

or nephews. Minnie, Johnnie, Noona, Cramond, Bob and Lou—all the children worked hard to win the prize. Lou, who was among the smallest, dictated his history to his mother every Sunday afternoon for five Sundays.

When the story itself was written, he drew pictures to illustrate it—pictures of the Children of Israel crossing the Red Sea with big suitcases in their hands, large cigars in their mouths, and tall silk hats on their heads, such as Papa wore when he went out! But one of the older children wrote a better history than Lou's, and won the prize. Uncle David, however, liked Lou's history so much that he gave him a special prize, a Bible story-book full of pictures, as a reward for writing about Moses.

On his birthday in November, Lou's aunt gave him a fine present—a toy theatre. With Bob he gave many plays in this theatre. Some of the plays were original, but more of them they bought in a shop in Leith Walk. This shop, at the corner of Antigua Street not far from Inverleith Terrace, was a landmark of Lou's childhood. It was here he came on Saturday afternoons, with his week's allowance in his pocket, to buy marbles and lollipops, or the precious paper-backed plays so full of thrills and adventure. The shop was kept by a Mr. Smith.

All the plays at Mr. Smith's shop belonged to one series, "Skelt's Juvenile Dramas," in which there was a great variety of separate titles. *Alladin, The Red Rover, Robin Hood, The Old Oak Chest, Three-Fingered Jack, The Blind Boy*—which of these should he buy? The plays cost a penny each when the illustrations were in black and white, two pennies (or tuppence, as they said), if the illustrations were in color. Lou and Bob preferred the uncolored pictures, so that they might color them themselves at home.

Lou often took so long in deciding which play he would have that Mr. Smith grew impatient.

"Hoots, noo, laddie," he would say, sweeping the pile of plays off the counter, "I ken ye mean never to buy at all."

"Oh, yes, Mr. Smith," Lou answered, "Yes, I do!"

"Let me see your money then."

Hastily Lou showed him his penny, after which Mr. Smith put the uncolored plays back on the counter.

"Make haste noo, laddie. Which is't to be?"

"The Blind Boy, I think, Mr. Smith."

And so, his choice made at last, he came out into the street hugging the new play under his arm.

From Mr. Smith's the boys sometimes walked all the way down Leith Walk to the sea—a distance of two miles. There was much to see along the way, more when they got down to the village of Leith on the shore. Boats lay in the little harbor there under the hard, gray sky. Sailors in rough clothes lounged on the docks. There was

25

a smell of tar and seaweed in the air, making everything seem different and romantic. With Bob beside him, Lou was no longer afraid of the sea.

After spending an hour or two at the harbor, however, he began to want to return home, so that he might color his new play before bedtime. Tea also was waiting, the hot tea and scones or crackers which were his supper most of the year around when he did not dine with his parents.

After tea the boys spread themselves out comfortably on the floor, their paints beside them. Bob, too, had a new book to color.

Lou asked an important question.

"The blind boy, Cummy, would he be wearing a ring?"

"Gravy, laddie, how do I ken? Gi' me the book here, and I'll tell ye."

Cummy read a few pages silently, moving her lips as she did so, and frowning a little, too, for she did not approve of play-acting.

"Ay, laddie, the boy was unfortunate, but he was a prince. He would be wearing a ring."

"Thank you, Cummy. And now," seeing that Cummy was folding up her sewing, "One mair picture before bed. It is so grand, the coloring."

"One mair, laddie, then."

Lou painted one more picture, and went to bed with the colors dancing before his eyes.

Chapter VI

My tea is nearly ready and the sun has left the sky,
It's time to take the window to see Leerie going by.
For every night at tea-time and before you take your seat,
With lantern and with ladder he comes posting up the street. Thank you, lady

MEANWHILE THE STEVENSON family had moved to a new home. From the smaller low-lying house in Inverleith Terrace they moved across the river and uphill nearer the business part of the city to a fine stone house opposite a pretty park. The name of the new street was Heriot Row; the number was 17. At 17 Heriot Row Lou spent all the rest of his boyhood and his college days.

The new home was in the heart of what was known as the New Town, that is, the newer, wealthier part of the city to the north of Castle Rock. On the south side of the Rock lay the Old Town—the dirty, forlorn part of the city, where the little children did not have rabbit-pie for dinner. On his walks with Bob and Cummy, Lou had

27

seen some of the dirty streets of the Old Town. As he grew older he learned more and more about them.

The park opposite the new house in Heriot Row was called Queen Street Gardens. There were trees and meadows there, where blackbirds sang, quantities of blooming lilac, and a round pond full of ducks. The children who played in the gardens sailed their boats in this pond. Sometimes the ducks went quacking after the boats, as they sailed across the water.

Behind the house in Heriot Row, where there might have been a small garden, there was a great litter of iron and other metal which Mr. Stevenson kept there for experimental purposes. A brighter and clearer light, one that revolved more smoothly, this was what he was forever trying to make.

Inside the new home at the top of the house Lou had comfortable rooms for his own use. A nursery or playroom, his bedroom, Cummy's room at the back. But no-one dreamed that he would spend as much time in his own rooms as he did during the next three years. The long months stretched out, and Lou was not well at all.

In September he tried going to school at a Mr. Henderson's around the corner, but he soon had to give that up. Coughs and colds and vague feverish illnesses distressed him. It was now apparent to everyone that the gay, imaginative Lou had weak lungs, that he must have careful nursing if he was to grow up into a man.

Years afterward he wrote about those days and nights in Heriot Row. How he lay in bed during the day, playing with his toys and coughing. How, when he was up at all, he sat at the window in the late afternoon, waiting for Leerie, the lamplighter, to come up the street with a ladder on his back and a lighted taper in his hand, with which to light the old-fashioned gas street-lamp in front of the house. How he lay in bed at night, coughing and unable to sleep, while the room seemed to swell and shrink around him.

There were times, too, when he had strange dreams and nightmares, in which he saw great crowds marching through the streets, heard curious music or the beat of horses' hoofs. A strange fear that the world was a big orange, which he must swallow, came over him. If the fire fell apart in the grate, or a loud crack came from the big cabinet in the corner, he started up, frightened and perspiring.

At such times his father came up from his bedroom downstairs to sit beside him. Lou clung to his father's hand, and watched his face in the firelight, while Mr. Stevenson told stories. These stories were about old sailors, inn-keepers, or coachmen his father had met in his travels. They were very soothing, consisting mostly of conversation.

"I said to the old coachman, 'That's a fine gray mare ye have there, Thomas'," his father would begin. "And then the old coachman said to me, 'I've driven many miles behind her, sir, and never failed to get there yet.' "

By and by the quaking Lou felt calmer, and sipped some cocoa or coffee Cummy made for him. But he could never understand why he felt so brave and full of adventure during the day, yet at night seemed small and frightened. It was many years before he learned not to feel small and frightened at night.

Perhaps one reason why he felt this way was because during the day he heard so many exciting stories. As the winter days grew darker, and he was more and more in the house, Cummy or his mother read to him a great deal. Lou liked stories of adventure, so they read about pirates and soldiers, giants stealing beautiful ladies, wild animals in the forest.

Nowadays it is doubtful whether a small, sickly child would be allowed to hear so many harrowing tales while he was ill in bed. Neither would he be given tea or coffee to drink when he could not sleep at night. Even the milk Lou drank might very well have been infected, since there were a great many tubercular cattle in those days and no law, such as there is now, requiring that all cows be tested. Yet he lived in a comfortable home, surrounded by every attention. A child today under those circumstances might not have been ill at all.

Meanwhile he had a new playmate who made the time pass much more quickly. Coolin, a round, fat puppy came to him shortly before his birthday in November. What a gift that was! A dog to run in the park with him when he was able to be out; to lie on the floor beside him when he was at home in bed; to lick his hand with his moist, pink tongue a dozen times a day! All through his boyhood Coolin remained his great friend and companion.

Chapter VII

The level of the parlour-floor
Was honest, homely, Scottish shore;
But when we climbed upon a chair
Behold the gorgeous East was there!

DURING THOSE YEARS when he was not well—in fact, from the time he was two months old until he was ten—Lou often stayed with his grandfather Balfour in the little village of Colinton four miles south of Edinburgh. Grandfather Balfour, or "Gatty" as Lou called him, lived in a house that sat on a low piece of ground between a hill and a river. On the side of the hill there was a church; it was here that Gatty preached every Sunday. On the other side of the house there was the river, curving around it like a big brown arm. The opposite bank of the river, which was heavily wooded, rose up steeply.

This river, Lou learned, was the same Water of Leith which flowed under the bridge at the end of Inverleith Terrace in town where he lived. How nice that was!

The river protected him; it went everywhere that he did! Boats launched on the river at Colinton must float bravely all the way to Edinburgh, while he himself drove in and out of town behind Gatty's old brown horse.

The house itself at Colinton was square and yellow. When the sun shone it seemed to sit, as he wrote later, in a cup of sunshine on the lawn. But when the weather was bad, as it was in November or March, water dripped from the eaves and made everyone glad to be indoors. Sometimes Lou was there for several weeks without being able to go outdoors at all.

This did not disturb him in the least, because the house itself was mysterious and fascinating. On coming into it from the drive, one entered a long, cool hall with a stone floor. To the right of this hall was the parlor, to the left Gatty's study, at the end the dining room. Against the wall in the hall stood a cabinet of varied treasures—stuffed birds, carved beans, bangles, bells, marble figures—all gifts to Grandfather or Aunt Jane from the four uncles who lived in India.

The dining room at the end of the hall was the room where Lou played. It was here also that Aunt Jane, who kept house for Gatty, did her sewing and housekeeping. Aunt Jane was a person whom everyone loved, although she was partly deaf and blind from an accident long ago. In her black silk dress and white shawl she moved around all day long making other people comfortable.

Besides her shawl and ear-trumpet, Aunt Jane always carried a large bunch of keys at her waist, one of which opened the storeroom at the end of the dining room. This storeroom was full of wonderful things. Long bars of soap like loaves of bread to be sliced into thick pieces, tin boxes of crackers, wooden racks of eggs, spices in funny jars, a fat, black jar of calves' foot jelly, which was Lou's special property. Every morning at eleven o'clock, when Lou was at Colinton, Aunt Jane unlocked the storeroom door and got out three round crackers, called Albert biscuits, and the jar of calves' foot jelly. Spreading the jelly on the crackers, she said that it would make him strong and handsome; it certainly tasted as if it would. Sometimes, too, when Lou had taken medicine, she got out a barley-sugar drop which she called a "tuckie," and gave him that.

Standing beside the dining room window with his tuckie in his hand, Lou could see the gardener outside, digging in the rain with the drops dripping off the edge of his hat. The hens, too, shook water out of their tails as they ran to meet the girl from the kitchen with her pan of scraps.

Going into the hall where the case of Indian things stood, Lou took out carefully the carved beans or the little marble god to play with. One day Gatty came out suddenly from his study, and found him there.

"Come into the study after tea, Lewis," he said, using Lou's baptismal name and looking at him sharply from under bushy white eyebrows. "I will show ye some more things which your uncles ha' sent from India. They are soldiers there, ye know."

"Ay," said Lou, "and when I grow up I shall be a soldier, too."

"Nonsense, laddie," said Gatty. "Ye are much too delicate for that. Always ailing and blowing. But come in after tea, and I will show ye the treasures."

Gatty went back into his study where he spent many hours each day writing letters or sermons, often drinking a glass of wine or eating nuts while he wrote. The study was filled with great religious books.

Lou could hardly wait until tea-time, and afterward knocked eagerly at the study door. But Gatty's thoughts were elsewhere that day; he scarcely seemed to know that Lou was there at all.

Going back into the dining room, where the fire glowed and the lamp was lighted, Lou crept behind the sofa and played that he was an explorer in a hostile country, crawling cautiously on hands and knees around an enemy village. The chairs and tables became native huts; Aunt Jane, sewing in the firelight, was the enemy chieftain. The ear-trumpet beside her on the table, which helped her to hear what people said, became a weapon.

35

So vividly did Lou imagine these things that when Cummy came to take him up to bed, he shrank back fearfully behind the sofa, believing that Aunt Jane really was an enemy. A moment later, however, he came out and threw his arms affectionately around her neck.

Chapter VIII

Bring the comb and play upon it!
Marching here we come!
Willie cocks his highland bonnet,
Johnnie beats the drum.

LATER IN THE SPRING, of course, when the weather was
better, he played out on the lawn in the sunshine. Colinton in springtime was enchanting. Birds sang and built
their nests in the laurel bushes beside the driveway; jon-
quils sprang into bloom on the green lawn; in the kitchen
garden behind the house the gardener bent over his
radishes; calves and colts followed their mothers around
the surrounding pastures; in the fields beyond the churchyard men were plowing steadily.

Lou had now no time for the Indian treasures in the
cabinet in the hall. All day long he ran around the green
lawn, watching the birds nesting, welcoming each new
flower as it opened.

Soon, too, some of his cousins came to stay with Aunt

37

Jane and Gatty. Lou had many cousins. From India alone, where the four uncles lived, there came many cousins, and there were others from near by as well.

When he was tired of playing on the lawn, Lou liked to creep under the evergreen trees at the corner, through a small gate in the wall, and down the sloping bank to the river, where the water flowed darkly under overhanging trees. Beyond where he was standing the old mill-wheel by the stable churned the water into foam.

With his cousin Minnie one day he crept thus down to the river. There they found a little island of yellow sand sticking up out of the dark water. Lou shouted boldly:

"A desert island! Let us capture it!"

"You go first," said Minnie doubtfully.

Lou's hair was damp and warm on his forehead.

"Here I go!" he cried, jumping down on the island.

But the soft sand was treacherous, beginning to give way beneath him.

"Here I come!" he cried, scrambling back on the bank again. Minnie stretched out a hand to him. The little island sank slowly from sight.

So they sat down on the bank and began to make boats out of the broad leaves of the butter-burs growing thickly along the bank. These leaves were large enough to hold a good piece of butter. The country people wrapped their butter in them before they took it to market. Fastened to a stick, the butter-burs made excellent sails for a boat, or weighted with a little sand, they became boats in themselves, sailing slowly down the river to the sea.

Other days, when there were still more cousins to play with, the children rode sticks up and down the paths for horses, or pretended to fight a giant, called Bunker, who was holding a princess in captivity at the far end of the garden. Sometimes, too, they held a parade, with dishpans for drums and napkins tied to sticks for flags and paper hats on their heads.

One thing they must remember when they were playing in the garden, and that was not to step on the plots of carefully-raked ground where flowers or vegetables had been planted. A fresh footprint on any of these was a grave matter in Grandfather Balfour's eyes. The children thought he looked for footprints after they were in bed at night, and measured any that he found. Then he was supposed to look upstairs outside the bedroom doors, where the shoes waited to be polished, for the shoe that fitted his measure.

Whether he did this or not, he certainly spoke sharply to any boy or girl who made a false step. It was Lou who discovered that if he made a slight swish with his foot when he stepped in the wrong place, the footprint would be longer than his shoe, and therefore somewhat misleading. He tried, however, not to step on the beds at all, because the flowers would soon be blooming there. In the kitchen garden, too, the gardener had planted radishes and lettuce and tomatoes.

This gardener was a strange man who seemed to dislike boys. He did not answer them when they spoke to him. At night, too, before he went home, he locked his tools up carefully in the toolhouse, so that no boy could take them out. Lou tried to get him to play soldiers with him, but he never would. He only sniffed and went on planting potatoes.

One thing the cousins liked to do was to talk over what they would be when they grew up. Lou still insisted that he would be a soldier. Henrietta said that she would be a baker so that she could have all the currant buns and ginger cake she wanted. Billy said that he would be a chimney sweep—one of those strange, sooty boys who came to the house once a year and actually climbed up into the chimneys to sweep them.

Meanwhile there was no end to the games they played together. One day when Lou was five, they found a clothes-basket in a cupboard under the stairs, and carried it out into the meadow to use as a boat. The wind rippling across the tall grass there made them think of waves. Using the basket for a boat, they played that they were shipwrecked sailors on a desert island, looking desperately for food. As there were no houses on the desert island, they could not go back to Gatty's house for something to eat. Finally Lou suggested that they eat butter-cups as the cows did. Moving slowly across the meadow, the cows ate the buttercups eagerly. The children believed that that was why their butter was yellow.

Billy and Lou ate several of the flowers. Henrietta said they were too bitter. But when they got back to the rectory the boys, and especially Lou, were very sick. Obviously buttercups did not agree with them at all.

Lying up in his small bedroom, next a large room with red curtains, Lou thought about this in some perplexity. The cows ate buttercups, and gave milk, which he could drink, and cream, which became yellow butter. Then why could he himself not eat the yellow flowers safely? It was very plain, however, that he could not. In future they must take their food with them when they went boating in the fields . . .

The sea, the town and the country. All three were now a settled part of Lou's background.

Chapter IX

Whenever Auntie moves around
Her dresses make a curious sound.
They trail behind her up the floor,
And trundle after through the door.

ONE MORNING AT Colinton when Lou had been playing down by the river with Henrietta, he came out on the lawn from under the evergreen trees to find all the furniture from the parlor set out on the grass. Aunt Jane, with a cloth over her head, was helping the girl to clean it.

The children walked round and round the familiar chairs and tables, finding them very strange in their new place on the lawn. Suddenly Lou pounced on something.

"Aunt Jane, Aunt Jane, what is this?" he shouted into her ear-trumpet, holding up an enormous white bone.

"The wingbone of an albatross, laddie. An albatross is a great bird."

"But where are they, Aunt Jane? I want to see one."

"Nae, nae, laddie. They are not in Scotland. They fly over the sea, following the ships, even sleeping in the air on a long flight. The sailors say they bring great luck to a ship. There is a fine poem about an old sailor who shot an albatross. It is called *The Ancient Mariner*.

"What does that mean, Auntie—ancient mariner?"

"It means 'old sailor.' The poem is about how much the sailor suffered after he killed the great bird."

"Sing it for me, Aunt Jane. Sing it for me."

"It is no' a song, it is a poem, laddie. I think I can say it for you—I used to know it by heart."

Aunt Jane put down her dust-cloth, and stood up very straight.

> " 'He was an ancient mariner,
>   And he stoppeth one of three.
>   *By thy long gray beard and glittering eye,*
>   *Now wherefore stoppest thou me?'* "

she began in a strong, clear voice.

The poem, which most school children today know and recite, told how the old sailor stopped a man in the street to tell him about the albatross he had shot. This bird, he said, flew behind his ship for days and became a great pet. Then one day for no good reason he shot the bird with his bow and arrow. From that day on the wind died down, the ship was becalmed and could go nowhere. Gradually all the sailors but the one telling the story died of thirst.

"Oh, Aunt Jane, did they all really die of thirst?"

"Well, that is the story, laddie."

"It is a fine story, Aunt Jane. I can tell stories, too. I tell myself stories when I go to sleep at night."

"That is fine, laddie. But ye maun go to sleep, too."

"Yes, Aunt Jane."

Lou slipped away quietly so he would not have to hear more about going to sleep at night. It was a subject which distressed him. All day, when he was playing out on the lawn, he thought that of course he would go to sleep at night. But once he was in his bed, with the gay coverlet over him and the pictures of soldiers at Sebastopol pasted around the wall, he never wanted to sleep. Tired and feverish though he was, he still wanted to tell himself stories. These stories he called "songstries"— since he sang many of them softly to himself as he told them.

No-one suspected that in these songstries lay the first sign of Lou's great talent as a story-teller. The other children did not make up stories at night. They went peacefully to sleep while he was still wide-awake and restless. Yet neither Mamma nor Papa Stevenson, Cummy nor Aunt Jane suspected that the boy who sang songstries at night would some day grow up to be a famous author. Even when he had been naughty, and had to stand in the corner, Lou made up stories, forgetting entirely that he was being punished, until Cummy pulled him around and kissed him.

Sometimes Lou was alone at Colinton, and then he played more quietly but no less intensely. For hours he lay in the laurel bushes at the corner of the lawn waiting for a red deer to come down the driveway. Popping away at this imaginary deer with his gun, he carried the carcass in to Aunt Jane in the dining room. When they had cold lamb for dinner later, they both said it was red venison with a fine flavor.

Aunt Jane was really a remarkable person. Although she could neither see nor hear well, she understood many things. Without anyone telling her she seemed to know when a boy or girl was ailing, if the strawberries were ripe in the garden, or if Gatty's horse had come into the driveway.

From her magic cupboard in the dining room she still pulled delightful things. Now that the currants were ripe and fresh jelly had been made, she often gave Lou a "jeely-piece" in mid-morning. A "jeely piece" was bread and butter spread with fresh jelly. These and her "tuckies" after taking medicine made Aunt Jane very popular with her nieces and nephews. Gatty himself got a tuckie after he had taken some bittter medicine which his failing health demanded.

It was while Lou was at Colinton with Aunt Jane,

when he was about eight years old, that he first began to read for himself. Before that other people had always read to him. Since he did not go to school, and had never studied reading systematically, it is not surprising that he was slow at learning to read.

But one summer day when he had been sent into the village on some errand, he carried a book of fairy-tales along with him. And coming home later through a fir-wood, careless of what was going on around him, he looked into the book and found that he could read most of the words. Odd words that he had learned helped him; Cummy had taught him some words, too. Without knowing that he was doing it, he had learned to read for himself!

After that he was soon reading many books, among them the *Arabian Nights Entertainment* in a fat volume with double columns of print down the pages. How he loved the story of Ali Baba and the forty thieves. When he ate his calves' foot jelly now, which he took from a saucer with a horn spoon, he dug a hole in the side of the jelly and pretended that it was the cave of the forty robbers.

Books which told of Scottish history pleased him very much, too. Scotland, he discovered, had had a very long and rich past as a nation. In the days before uniting with England, when Scotland was a kingdom all its own, many brave men had died protecting the Scottish kings.

Many wars, too, had been fought over who should be the king. One of the bravest kings of Scotland was named Robert, the Bruce. Another young prince, who tried to become king but failed, was called Bonny Prince Charlie.

Then there had been much trouble in Scotland over religious questions. This caused the bitterest fighting of all. People from outside tried to tell Scottish men and women what kind of church service they should have. Different groups of people inside Scotland disagreed about church matters. For years in different periods of Scottish history battles had been fought over these questions.

Lou read about these battles in historical books written for boys. *Little Arthur's History of England; Peter Parley's Historical Tales;* Walter Scott's *Tales of a Grandfather;* a book called *Harry's Ladder to Learning.* From these, and other books, he learned how Robert, the Bruce, fought to make Scotland a strong kingdom. He also learned that they did not use guns in the early wars, but fought with bows and arrows, and spears, and hatchets with long handles which were called pikes by the soldiers.

School Days

Chapter X

Late lies the wintry sun a-bed,
A frosty, fiery sleepy-head;
Blinks but an hour or two; and then,
A blood-red orange, sets again.

IN THE AUTUMN before he was nine, Lou began again to go to school—not as other boys went, regularly every day, but sometimes, when he was well enough. In a Scotch cap with a tassle, and a vest buttoned up high on his chest, he went when he could to Mr. Henderson's School in India Street around the corner from his home.

How hard it was for Lou to become a schoolboy. The hothouse atmosphere of his nursery had not prepared him for playing roughly with other boys. When they played cricket or football, he shrank away from the playground. When they invented new games and adventures, however, he led all the others.

The first two years of school he did not make friends as he should have. Reading, painting, writing were still

51

the things he loved best, although he bristled with anger when the boys called him "softie" and snatched his cap off his head. Too often he ran away home to his books and paints, when he might have been happier learning how to make friends at school.

In his father's library were many books he could now understand and enjoy. This library was a silent, solemn room; when he was younger he did not like to go there. As a schoolboy, however, he dug into the shelves, passing over books on lamps and lighting and engineering, sermons in Latin, scientific encyclopedias, until he came to stories of adventure. *The Voyages of Captain Woodes Rogers,* a great traveler; a history of that famous English fortress, the Tower of London; four bound volumes of the magazine, *Punch,* full of jokes and funny pictures.

Lying on the floor with these treasures, he read for hours at a time, living a most exciting life in his mind. When he was not actually reading, he made up stories of his own in which he imagined himself digging for gold, shipwrecked on a desert island, or saving beautiful ladies from pirates. He also drew, painted, and cut out actors for his toy theatre.

Much of the time during these years his mother was ill, and he must amuse himself. It was a great grief to him when his dog, Coolin, was killed in a fight, but soon after, another Coolin was given to him.

Both Lou and his father were very fond of dogs.

Walking on the street, Mr. Stevenson often stopped to talk to stray dogs, so that the dogs came to know him. One dog, named Bob, waited at a certain corner for him every afternoon, hoping that Mr. Stevenson would come by and buy him a meat pie in a shop, which he sometimes did.

Lou admired his father very much in some ways, but he was troubled by his sternness. Facts and figures meant so much to Papa. Pictures and stories did not. It was hard for Lou to talk to Papa about them.

Toward the end of the year, when the days became shorter, a lovely powdery snow fell frequently during the afternoon. This snow made Lou more willing to play outdoors. The boys in Queen Street Gardens were making snowballs or running races with their long woolen mufflers streaming out behind. Lou did not often join them, but he watched their games with pleasure. In the shop windows on Prince's Street at this time, too, tempting New Year's cakes were on display. Lou loved the great pans of Scotch bun, a special New Year's treat, with the crust cracking open around the edges, so that he could see the raisins and spices inside.

At New Year's time each year the postman and Leerie, the lamplighter, left verses at the kitchen-door, saying they had done their work faithfully during the last twelve months. The cook gave these verses to Mr. Stevenson, who read them aloud at dinner, and on New Year's

Day a present of money, called a "handsel" was waiting for the postman and the lamplighter.

Lou himself usually got half-a-crown (about sixty cents) for a New Year's Day present. What a treat that was! Visiting the shops one by one, he took the whole afternoon to decide how to spend it. Should he buy something sweet to eat—a piece of Scotch bun or barley-sugar—or should he buy new paints, or a present for his mother? Sometimes it was a book which attracted him.

Meanwhile, no one could pretend that his work at school was going well. Two years had gone by since he began to go to Mr. Henderson's. His teachers complained that he did not come often enough, or work hard enough, to know what his lessons were about. This did not upset his family as much as it might have. His mother and Cummy wanted most of all to keep him well. His father said that practical experience later would teach him what a lighthouse-builder needed to know. On the whole, however, it seemed wise to send him to another school. So the following autumn, when he was almost eleven, he began to go to a larger school, called the Edinburgh Academy.

The Edinburgh Academy was built on a low piece of ground down near the Water of Leith. The building itself looked like a Greek temple. All around the building was a gravel yard, in which the boys played and shouted out of school hours. On his way to school Lou, like all the other boys, carried a wooden racket, called a "clacken." These clackens they rattled against the iron railings of the houses which they passed. The game was to make as much noise with a clacken as possible.

Lou set out for school in a brave flourishing manner. Always in his own mind he was a prince or a soldier: some fine fellow out to do brave deeds. But when he got to the schoolyard this confidence in himself somehow faded. He did not know how to show the other boys what a fine fellow he was.

Disappointed, he wandered a good deal by himself away from the schoolyard. The Craigleith stone-quarry, near the Queensferry Road going down to the sea, made a fine place to play. Far down in the great holes in the rock, green water glittered. The road near-by led down to the fishing-village of Queensferry, where boats lay in the harbor and the streets were full of sailors in rough clothes.

Another place where Lou liked to go was up around the Castle. So much Scottish history had been centered around this fortress. The rocky ridge on which it stood rose up sharply against the sky. Below the ridge on one side, there were pretty public gardens, on the other, a group of damp slum houses. The sides of the ridge itself were rocky and very steep; to reach the Castle one climbed up the backbone of the great rock, like walking up a sleeping animal from the tail to the head.

Once on a fine afternoon Lou climbed up to the Castle at the west end, the steepest side of the hill, and laid his hand on the rampart. The afternoon sun, red and splendid, warmed his back as he climbed.

But before he had been at the Academy long enough to settle down and make friends among the boys, Lou's father became ill and the whole family went away to the south of England. Once more he was back in the familiar hothouse atmosphere of his family, with Cummy always at hand to wait on him. The thin and nervous Lou with the active mind must still learn to be a boy among boys.

Chapter XI

Sing a song of seasons!
Something bright in all!
Flowers in the summer!
Fires in the fall!

THAT SUMMER AFTER they returned from England, the Stevenson family rented a furnished house at the seashore. It was no longer possible now to go to Colinton. The old home there was broken up. Grandfather Balfour had died, and another clergyman and his family lived in the dear yellow house.

The seashore, however, was an admirable substitute. The village where they rented the house was called North Berwick. It was built on a little point of land sticking out into the ocean, about ten miles from Edinburgh. The village itself consisted of two long streets of red houses. The houses which the summer visitors rented stretched along the shore to the right and left of the village.

There was everything at North Berwick to make a boy happy. The blue sea full of rocks and little islets; pools of sea-water on the shore in which to fish; rocks and crags to climb on; the crashing water in which to bathe. Behind the town there was a golf-links full of rabbit-holes. Overhead the sea-gulls cried.

Here with his cousins and the neighborhood boys Lou spent an active summer. During the earlier part of his stay the favorite game was one called "Crusoeing." "Crusoeing" consisted of eating out-of-doors in what-ever way one could without help from home. Sometimes the boys brought apples, and, hidden away in a sheltered place on the shore, built a fire of dried seaweed and roasted them. Sometimes they gathered sour, wild cher-ries, called "geans", from a tree along the coast, and ate them as shipwrecked, starving men might do, right off the tree.

Toward the end of September came the best game of all—one that required the cool, darkish nights of Sep-tember. This game was called "Lantern-bearing." As the colder weather approached, each boy bought himself a tin ship's-lantern, with a metal slide that might be drawn over the opening. Thus the lantern could be carried with-out a ray of light showing, although it smelled badly at such times and often went out.

Every night after tea the boys lighted their lanterns,

58

closed the slides, buckled the lanterns to their leather cricket belts under their coats, and went out to find their friends. The game was to walk about without a crack of light showing, until one met another lantern-bearer.

When two of them met, the first one said in a low, meaningful voice,

"Have you got your lantern?"

"Yes."

"Let us go and find another."

Gradually a party of lantern-bearers formed in the silent streets, and turned down toward the shore. Here a pit had been dug in the sand, large enough to hold all the boys. In the pit the boys seated themselves in a circle with their lanterns in the middle. Then they told each other ghost-stories as long as they dared to stay out.

What stories Lou told on those nights, his brown eager face lighted by the lanterns. What fun he had thinking up the stories all the day long.

When they separated to go home, each boy hid his light carefully before going up the village street.

The end of September, of course, put an end to the lantern-bearing. The boys must go back to town to begin a new school year. Lou went, like all the others, back to school, but his attendance was irregular. No one urged him to study his lessons. His father still said that book-learning was of small use to an engineer.

59

Since his family felt as they did about his lessons, it was easy for Lou to spend a good deal of time writing stories instead of studying. The boys at North Berwick had liked his stories. He would put some of them in a magazine which the boys at school might read at a penny a number. This magazine he called *The Schoolboys' Magazine*.

One issue of the magazine still survives. It contains four thrillers, the first one, which was to be continued, ended with the hero hidden inside a boiler under which a fire had been lighted. The second was about a wounded man hidden under the floor in a deserted castle. The third began with two evil-looking men standing beside a shipwreck at North Berwick. The fourth told how two sailors in the South Seas were captured by natives, and ordered burned alive.

Meanwhile, neither Lou nor his mother was very well. The weather had grown steadily worse, and it affected them both. A dozen times a day it rained or snowed. By evening gray sea-fogs blew inland and wrapped the city in mist. Mrs. Stevenson and Lou coughed in the night, so that Cummy must be up many times getting hot milk or coffee to quiet them.

In January Mr. Stevenson decided suddenly that something must be done about his family. They must all go abroad to the south of France—to Nice where the sun was shining and the air was warm. Suitcases and bundles were hastily got together, a roll of steamer-rugs made ready. On the morning of the day they left, Cummy called them all early. By ten o'clock they were in the fast train for London, rolling rapidly along the frozen coast of Scotland.

Chapter XII

Great is the sun, and wide he goes
Through empty heaven without repose;
And in the blue and glowing days
More thick than rain he showers his rays.

BY THE EVENING of January seventh they were in Paris, eating a fine French dinner at the hotel. Chops and stewed carrots to start with, then chicken and mashed potatoes. How seldom Lou had eaten two meat courses in one dinner! After them came French pastry, which Scottish people call "shapes," followed by fresh pears as big as Lou's two hands.

Cummy and Lou liked France. They had never seen so many mirrors anywhere. In the restaurants, in the hotels, everywhere there were fine mirrors with gold frames.

Continuing their journey south from Paris, they began to see more country-people—priests in long black coats with white gowns underneath them, peasants in thick wooden shoes, the toes of which had been brightly painted. Cummy did not like France so well now, because she could not get a cup of tea in the afternoon. Above her tightly-buttoned waist, with its high collar around her throat, her face looked pale and tired. But she looked after her invalids carefully, no matter how she felt, with untiring devotion.

Coming into Marseilles they began to feel the warmth of a more southern climate. Olive trees and vineyards grew on the dusty hills in the sun. From Cannes they drove in a carriage, drawn by five horses, over a rough road on the edge of a precipice overlooking the sea. How blue and deep it was! The sun was now so strong that men carried yellow or white umbrellas over their heads. In the rivers along the shore, women washed their clothes on the round smooth stones.

On the fifteenth of January, eleven days after they had left Scotland, they reached their journey's-end at Nice. The hotel there was white and glistening. In the court yard before it, orange trees had been planted in tubs, and people sat at little tables, sipping wine. When they went down to dinner later, fifty people sat down together at a long table down the center of the dining room. Lou broke his bread into his soup, as he saw other people doing, and wondered what the French words for soup and bread were.

For six weeks they stayed at the hotel in Nice. Sometimes Lou must go down to dinner alone, because his mother was not well. During the day he and Cummy wandered about the town, or up into the hills, or down by the sea. How strange to see the sun shining warm and bright in January, to sit out-of-doors, to watch the windmills turning in the gentle breeze. Lou loved the windmills. At night he saw them turning slowly in his sleep. Both he and Cummy learned to say a great many French words—water, milk, bread, cheese, soup, sugar.

Late in February the Stevenson family took a house at Mentone for two months. There the family dined by themselves every night on a dinner sent in by the confectioner. Lou loved the French pastries, filled with custard or cream and powdered with sugar. Cummy, however, liked best of all the cup of good Scotch tea, which she made for herself every night in this strange land.

Lou himself was in the finest spirits. Violets were blooming in Mentone; he could go out to pick them. From the front windows of the house he could see fishermen hauling in their nets. A shepherd with his flock sat all day on a hillside beside the house. Lou made friends with him, and learned to call the sheep in French.

A tutor came in mornings to give him lessons, but in the afternoon he and Cummy were free to wander anywhere. They discovered many interesting things on their walks. Lou was delighted with a plant, called a milk-plant, which grew beside the road. When one broke

64

open the stems or leaves of this plant, a white milky-looking liquid poured out.

One day they crossed a small bridge and found that they were no longer in France but in Italy. Leaving the road, they sat down in a lemon grove, so that Lou might draw pictures of the people who passed—women in broad hats, carrying baskets, men riding on little donkeys. Another day they climbed up into the hills where the olives grew, and tasted them green from the trees. Cummy did not like them. There were times when she was very wistful for a piece of oatbread or Scotch bun.

In April the family made a tour into Italy, visiting Genoa, Naples, Rome, and Florence. This trip was not altogether successful. Some of the time Lou was feverish; often his mother was too tired to go out. Cummy complained that she had walked so much that her feet felt as if they had been stewed. Toward the end of May they turned homeward again, reaching Calais on a cool night when a fire in the hotel sitting-room felt very good after months in a hot country. Lou loved an open fire. He was glad to see one again.

When the family reached London, Lou went north to Scotland alone, a long day's-journey in the train. It was wonderful to draw into the great empty station at Edinburgh, to see the castle on its rock still rising above the city. Wonderful, too, to reach his own doorstep, where Coolin, the second or third (for there was always a

65

Coolin at the Stevenson home now) welcomed him wildly. Leaping and jumping, the little dog followed him up to his bedroom where he went to wash his hands. Downstairs in the dining room, he licked his shoes again and again.

The next morning, however, Coolin showed signs of wanting to leave him. Before Lou had finished his breakfast, the dog ran to the door, whining.

"Stay home, Coolin," said Lou. "The cook will bring you a piece of fish when she comes from market."

Coolin leaped and barked, to show that he under stood about the fish, but still he stood at the door, whining. Lou got his cap and went out to see what Coolin wanted. As soon as the door was open, Coolin leaped up the street toward the uncle's house where he had stayed while Lou was gone. Did he want then to stay at the uncle's? Lou was a little anxious.

When they reached the uncle's house, Coolin ran upstairs eagerly to the nursery where there were two little cousins. In a few minutes, he came running down again, wagging his tail to show that he was ready to go home. The uncle's cook said that he had stolen a whole goose while Lou was gone, as well as several other pieces of food, when no-one was looking.

After that Coolin went every morning to visit the children at the other house, then came running briskly home again to get his piece of fish from the kitchen.

Chapter XIII

There stood the son and father
And they looked high and low;
The heather was red around them,
The sea rumbled below.

THAT SUMMER AT Peebles, twenty-five miles south of
Edinburgh on the River Tweed, Lou fished and swam
and wrote stories.

In the autumn, when they got back to Edinburgh, his
father talked of sending him away to school. His mother,
however, did not want him to go. Tears came into her
eyes whenever the subject was mentioned. Cummy, too,
laid out his woolen underwear on the bed, and wiped
her eyes when she saw it.

As a result, Lou himself began to wonder if he wished
to go away to school. The separation from home loomed
long and difficult. Thinking anxiously about it, he
walked one day alone on the London road, a road said
to be a thousand years old, certainly a road leading far

away from home. There was nothing alive in sight on the road as he trudged along save a cat who came out of a doorway and followed him.

Seeing the cat and the lonely road, Lou sat down suddenly on a doorstep and burst into tears. He felt that if he went away to school he would never be happy again, although he had often been so before, and at his age—not quite thirteen—might well expect a great many pleasant experiences. Seeing his tears, the cat came up and rubbed his legs, even jumped a little from side to side to attract his attention. Lou took her up in his arms, and wiped his eyes miserably on the fur on her back. When he did this, the cat jumped out of his arms hastily, and sat down a little way off to watch him. Apparently no one had ever cried into her fur before. Her expression, however, was sympathetic, so that Lou finally felt comforted and got up to go home.

That evening at dinner he told his family about the cat in the London Road. It was only on account of her that he mentioned his tears. His father listened to the story with astonishment.

"You did greet (cry) on the public highway, laddie, before a' the wurrld?" he asked over and over. "Then it is plain to me that ye ha' been too much wi' women. I shall take ye wi' me to the north on the lighthouse ship, away from petticoats . . ."

And so it was that young Lou made his first journey

on the lighthouse ship that went each year on a tour of inspection to the lighthouses and deep-ringing bells along the shores of Scotland.

The region which he and his father visited that year was the peninsula of Fife to the north and east of Edinburgh along a rocky coast. A number of small seaside villages lay along this peninsula, each with its tiny harbor protected by rocky islands in the sea. St. Andrews, Anstruther Wester, Anstruther Easter, Fair Isle, and a dozen other villages they visited, so that Mr. Stevenson might inspect the lighthouses.

At every stop the procedure was the same. The boat from the ship rowed ashore. The lighthouse-keeper stood on the beach in his uniform. Mr. Stevenson entered the lighthouse and began at once to climb the tower, noticing if the brass handrail was polished, the glass reflector clean of spray and oil, the extra lamp ready for instant use, the storm-windows at hand in case of need. If they were not, he frowned a great deal and talked earnestly with the keeper, who stood hot and embarrassed in his thick coat.

While his father was inspecting the lights, Lou hung about on the beach with his hands in his pockets, looking for a boy to play with, or thinking that in the town of Largo on this very peninsula there once lived a man named Andrew Selkirk, whose adventures on a desert island inspired Daniel Defoe to write the story of Robinson Crusoe. To Lou, the existence of the man, Selkirk, was much more important than the condition of the lighthouses. As long as there were practical men like his father to look after the lights, he preferred to let his thoughts wander over subjects like writing or adventure. This did not altogether please his father who had never read many books of adventure.

In one day on that trip, Mr. Stevenson visited seventeen lights along the rocky gray coast of the peninsula. To Lou it seemed amazing that so many lights could be needed. If Fife alone had so many lights, how many were there around the whole coast of Scotland? His father doubted if they had ever been counted.

When they got back home to Edinburgh, Mr. Stevenson insisted that Lou be packed off immediately to a boys' boarding school near London. His mother was going back to Mentone on account of her health; Cummy would probably go with her. Like Lou himself, Mrs. Stevenson had weak lungs. She needed sunshine and fresh air away from the cold winds of Scotland.

Lou was not at all happy in the school at Spring Grove. The boys there seemed to think only of football and cricket, which he could not play well, or of things to eat, which he liked better although he liked books and writing better still. In the dead of night they used to get up and eat sardine suppers by the light of a candle.

Lou ate the sardines greedily enough, but his throat

was often sore and he seemed far away from home. In the end, he wrote his parents such an appealing letter that they took him out of school and had him join them in Mentone for Christmas.

Lou was now a bookish boy of thirteen who had hardly ever been to school; who carried one book in his pocket to read and another to write in; who walked more often with Cummy than with boys of his own age; who asked his tutors so many questions about historical and romantic characters they hardly had time to teach him Latin or mathematics.

What kind of man would this thin, excitable boy make? Would he ever be willing to study engineering, so that he could draw diagrams and plan the building of harbor-lights?

Chapter XIV

. . . In the morning the shadow of the prison
turrets, and of many tall memorials, fall
upon the graves. There, in the hot fits
of youth, I came to be unhappy.

IN THE AUTUMN of 1864, when Lou was nearly fourteen, both he and his mother felt very much better. The family decided, therefore, to spend the winter in Edinburgh and to send Lou to Mr. Thompson's School in Frederick Street, across the gardens from Heriot Row. Mr. Thompson's school was very small; sometimes not more than a dozen boys attended in one term. All the studying was done at the school itself to make sure the work was covered. Mr. Thompson specialized in helping boys who were behind to catch up and get ready for college.

Even with this program Lou did not take his school-work very seriously, a fact which grieved Cummy. Now that he was better, she wanted him to take prizes, bring home medals, shine in Latin and mathematics. Lou did learn a good deal of French at Mr. Thompson's, but his spelling and grammar were terrible! His teachers said that he was bright and quick, but not very steady.

Meanwhile, he was quite happy. This was chiefly because he was busy writing. During that winter he wrote a great deal of foolish verse, which pleased him enormously. He also wrote the libretto for an opera called *The Baneful Potato*. There was a gardener in this opera, called "Dig-him-up-o," and a policeman called "Seek-him-out-o." Outside of school hours he read feverishly, novels about Scottish history by Sir Walter Scott and stories about the Covenanters, those heroic men of Scotland who were so persecuted because of their religious beliefs.

On the whole, it was a good school year. Lou did make up some lost ground, and he did make some friends.

When summer came, he and his family went back to Peebles on the River Tweed. Peebles was a town with many historical associations. Cromwell had attacked it during the wars between England and Scotland; portions of the town wall and cellars, where fugitives had hidden, still remained. There was a castle on the hill, now open to the winds, which had once been attacked by the invaders.

Lou bought himself a great thick cudgel, and strode up and down the hills, shaking it at imaginary enemies.

73

He also rode a brown pony, called "Purgatory." The boy who rode with him had a black pony which he called "Hell." The boy's sister, who also rode with them, called her pony "Heaven," and she followed them a little fearfully on their reckless rides. Once they rode, screaming and shouting, through the River Tweed itself to the little girl's great fright.

Other days they rowed on the Tweed, or waded in it. Quiet animals lived in the water or under the river's banks—water-rats, water-birds, fish, and frogs. The open-air life did Lou a great deal of good. He came back to town brown and hardy for the winter.

But the next two winters, and many winters after them, did not go well for Lou. Strange moods hung over him. One moment he was full of good-humor, excitement and fun; the next he felt distinctly unhappy.

He was a boy fifteen years old now—too old to cut down chairs for dragons in his nursery. Neither was it enough that his mother and Cummy adored him; he wanted people outside his home to admire him. Yet he was not very popular at school, and the thought of becoming an engineer lay like a lump in his chest.

In these moods, he wandered much by himself, a habit which grew on him. Off to the east of Castle Rock, there was another hill, called Calton Hill, with some bare pillars from an unfinished building standing forlornly on top of it. On the side of the hill there was a graveyard; below it a prison. In his helpless, moody fashion Lou climbed Calton Hill often in those days.

Lingering in the graveyard, he read the names on the tombstones and wondered what it was like to be no longer alive. Often he watched the grave-diggers digging new graves, while the birds watched the newly-turned earth for worms, and stray cats of the district watched the birds hungrily. It was not a cheerful thing to do, nor a very helpful one, excepting as it allowed him to think his thoughts in peace and gather his hopes together again for the morrow.

When he was tired of wandering in the graveyard, he sometimes climbed a stairway cut in solid rock to the top of the hill, where sheep fed quietly on the green turf growing up between the monuments. The view from the top of the hill was superb. Sea, city, sky, and clouds spread out before him. He could see the green suburbs, white roads winding down to the sea, troops marching on Castle Rock. If it were noontime when he was there, he could hear the great gun boom out at the Castle.

Lou wanted something on Calton Hill without knowing what it was.

Later on in the winter, when it was too cold to wander on Calton Hill, he lingered in the shabby district at the foot of the hill, where the pavements were always wet with rain, and cold, hungry people gathered in the dirty taverns to drink beer, or eat fish and potato chips, or soup with bread and pickles. These taverns, called public-houses, were not very respectable. Beggars, chimney-sweeps, men out of work, gathered there. At the bare tables one could buy a bowl of soup for a farthing (half a cent).

Slipping in quietly, Lou sat silently in the corner, watching the steam from the hot room collect on the window. In his pocket he carried a penny notebook in which to write verses. The men and women around him looked at him first with amazement; after a while they made friends with him. They knew that he was not a poor boy, although his clothes were untidy and he did not seem to have much money. Nevertheless, it was apparent that he did not belong there on a bench in The Green Elephant, or The Twinkling Eye, munching a pickle and shuffling his feet on the sanded floor. Just why he came, no-one—not even Lou himself—could say.

When his father heard about Lou's habit of visiting the public-houses, he reduced his pocket money to a very small sum. For years he kept him on such a small allowance that he was often embarrassed for money. But Lou continued to wander in strange streets and make friends with rough men and dirty children. At this time of his life nothing could make a happy boy out of him.

Chapter XV

Far from the loud sea beaches
Where he goes fishing and crying,
Here in the inland garden
Why is the sea-gull crying?

DURING THE SUMMER and early fall of the year 1866, Lou wrote a novel about the defeat of the Covenanters on a hillside not far from Colinton. The novel described vividly the death of brave, desperate men, and Lou was proud of it, but his father said the book lacked facts. He said that it should contain a great deal more historical information.

Mr. Stevenson's mind worked in this practical way. He could not look at the waves pounding along a rocky shore without counting the waves in order to estimate the depth of the water, or studying the ripples to see at what point a hidden reef was most dangerous. This way of thinking made him a great engineer. In the same way, in reading about a battle, he wanted to know how many men fought, and if they fought with swords or pistols, and how many horses there were in the attacking party, and if any cannon were fired. Lou struggled to make him see the human side of the story but could not. So he revised his novel into a sober pamphlet, called *The Pentland Rising,* which he thought very dull, but it pleased his father.

The result was that Mr. Stevenson had the pamphlet published in the fall. It contained twenty pages, and sold for sixpence (about twelve cents) in a few book-shops. Lou looked at it with pride. A published book of his own! When there were ten more like it he would be a successful writer whom everyone would admire and envy.

The winter passed and Lou finished his course at Mr. Thompson's School. In the fall he would be going up to the University, across the city in the Old Town, but he did not like to think of that. The University meant studying engineering, a profession which he did not like at all. To please his father, however, he pretended to like it, and scribbled as often as he could in a penny notebook in The Green Elephant.

In May, when the world was waking up to spring, his father rented a cottage in the country. This cottage was at Swanston, in the hills south of Edinburgh, two miles from Colinton where he had spent so many happy weeks as a boy. Feeling as he did about Colinton, it was natural that he should find Swanston wonderful, too. Buried away among the hills, it was like a different world from Edinburgh.

The cottage itself, a white, rambling farmhouse, nestled in a little dell with trees all around it. Tucked away behind it was the gardener's thatched cottage. Straight up beside the cottage rose the Pentland hills, treeless and grassy, dotted in the springtime with feeding sheep and lambs. Curlews cried up over the sheep; gulls, come inland from the ocean to feed behind neighboring plows, uttered strange cries. Over the hill lay the little village of Swanston itself, a tiny row of whitewashed cottages, with a bird-cage before nearly every door, and old ladies in white caps coming out to tend them.

The gardener at Swanston was like the gardener at Colinton: he didn't like to talk. Digging solemnly among the potatoes or cabbages in his old brown coat and stained hat, he seemed happy and at home, almost like a vegetable himself.

Vegetables were to him the finest things on earth. Because the mistress insisted, he did grow some flowers— bachelor's buttons, lady's-smock, hollyhocks, and roses— but these he scorned in his heart. When someone praised his cabbages or turnips, however, he touched his cap in gratitude, and quoted some verse from the Bible.

But the tall, scarecrowish Lou with the restless legs could not make friends with him as he wished. So he wandered idly among the hills, watching the sheep and carving a design on a bit of stick, or his initials on a golf ball.

One day on the hillside, he was startled by an immense gruff voice bellowing at him,

"C'way oot amang the sheep."

The man who spoke thus was John Todd, the shepherd. John had a red, weathered face, and carried a plaid shawl over his shoulder and a yellow staff under his arm. His dog, who helped him drive the sheep where he wanted them, trotted obediently at his heels.

Lou was a little afraid of John at first with his rough voice, but after a while he got used to him. The two became friends, and went out to look after the sheep in the evening together. John told him stories of sheepdogs, and how they could tell their master's sheep anywhere and drive them wherever the master wished them to go.

He also told him of battles which had been fought long ago on the very ground on which they stood. The farmhouse, he said, had been raided in 1845 by a group of rebellious Highlanders in search of food, who carried away a whole churnful of cream.

John was an old man, and an honest one. The boy, Lou, liked to walk with him at Swanston.

A Restless Young Man

Chapter XVI

Do you remember—can we e'er forget?—
How in the coiled perplexities of youth,
In our wild climate, in our scowling town,
We gloomed and shivered, sorrowed, sobbed and feared?

AUTUMN CAME; THE time to begin work at the University of Edinburgh. And work at the University meant studying to be an engineer, a lighthouse builder.

Striding forth from home one early November morning, Lou crossed the Queen Street Gardens to Prince's Street, and from there crossed the North Bridge to the Old Town. A half mile east through the grimy, shivery streets brought him to the weathered buildings of the University. This day he must begin to study Latin and mathematics, physics and moral philosophy—all the cold, hard subjects he hated, instead of English and French and history and poetry. Just why an engineer's son should dislike engineering so much it is hard to say, but the fact remained that Lou did. Nevertheless, for his father's sake he meant to study it.

The classrooms at the University were large and plain. The students sat on benches. The more elegant young men wore gloves; the country boys came in rough clothes. The professors wore cutaway coats with tails, and were very dignified.

Coming from his father's home, Lou should have been fashionably dressed. He wasn't. An old velvet lounging jacket, a flannel shirt, pepper-and-salt trousers, a muffler, such was his costume. He was quick, nervous, hurried, pale and very thin. His cough, which he called his "donkey's bray," rang out. Unless he felt very fresh and bright and well, he never came to his classes at all.

Friends came to this queer boy slowly. He felt bottled-up and feverish with ideas, poetry, and talk. But who was there to talk to?

His first year at the University was not very happy. How could it be when he was as cold as he was to what he was doing? Engineering had an open-air side to it which he loved. But all the long winter, he knew, his father went daily to a drab office and sat at a desk figuring out weights, measures and reflections of light rays, drawing plans with a ruler. A good engineer loves his ruler, a painter his brushes; Lou loved new pencils and notebooks.

During his second year at the University, he was more at a loose-end than ever. His old habit of wandering about in churchyards and slums came back to him. The older sections of Edinburgh were full of the most appalling slums—great, damp buildings, called "lands," in which poor people lived the most miserable of lives. If one did not cross from the New Town to the Old by one of the bridges, one climbed up long streets of such houses, so steep that the sidewalk was a flight of stone steps.

Not far from the University was an old church called Grayfriar's, which had an unusual graveyard where Lou liked to wander. This graveyard was always swarming with cats. It also had a great many curious gravestones, which Lou examined carefully. The sexton of this graveyard became Lou's friend. Smoking his pipe solidly, he dug the graves and shrubbery, while Lou lounged, talking, beside him. Around them rose the tenements where, through the open windows, they could see men eating their dinners, babies crying, women hanging out clothes high up in the air.

As he wandered around the churchyard or the gloomy streets, Lou always had a book stuffed in his pocket. Sometimes he read French novels of adventure; more often he read poetry, Keats and Swinburne during the first year, later Spenser, Wordsworth, and the Scottish Bobbie Burns, all rich, sweet poets who wrote of love and natural beauty, without any bone and steel in their philosophy. One melted along with them. Life was often sad, sometimes sweet, quite unmanageable. Lou, too, wrote poems about soft, sad things—dreams, skies, bird-songs.

When he was tired of wandering on the streets, he still ate in the disreputable taverns at the foot of Calton Hill. This was partly because he liked their gloomy atmosphere, partly because he had so little money to spend. Short of pocket-money, at times very bitter about it, since his father was quite a wealthy man, he considered pawning his watch or begged his mother secretly for extra money so that he could come and go more as he pleased.

Sometime during his second year at the University he changed the spelling of his name from Lewis to Louis. From Robert Lewis Balfour Stevenson he became Robert Louis Balfour Stevenson. Later he dropped the Balfour, and became Robert Louis Stevenson, although his friends always called him Louis Stevenson with the "s" pronounced, a variation from the French pronunciation.

During February of that year, 1869, he joined a debating society at the University, called the Speculative Society or "Spec.," but he did not go to many of their meetings. For weeks he stayed away from his classes. Often during those days he was cross and bad-tempered. His family did not know quite what to do with him.

It was only when his cousin, Bob, came home from studying art in France that he was able to shake off his gloomy moods for long at a time. Bob enjoyed nonsense, a hearty laugh. He liked to visit gay places in the New Town, not churchyards and slums. Taking Lou with him, he made him feel differently about his dull life as a student of engineering.

His summers as a student of engineering were spent actually watching engineering works being built. The summer that he was seventeen he spent the month of July up on the east coast of Scotland at a little town called Anstruther, where a breakwater was being built. After that he went on to another coast town, Wick, for six weeks to study another breakwater.

At Anstruther he lived with Bailie Brown, the carpenter, who, he said, gave him too many potatoes and too little fruit to eat, and no good place in which to write. The writing was all done at night in his bedroom by the light of two candles. The moths came in the open window, flew into the flame of his candles, and fell dead on the paper. Who could write under conditions like that?

By day he was out on the rough sea, pulling at ropes with blistered hands, watching the men work on the unfinished breakwater, loving the sea and the sea-smell and the glitter of diver's helmets under the water.

Wick, the second town he visited, he found to be nothing but a fishermen's village, built on bare rocks. The town reeked of herrings. The men who lived there thought of nothing but herrings. There were no fields or trees in the town at all—only slate fences, slate yards, slate roof on the houses. When two men met on the streets in this town, they said, "Breezy, breezy," to each other, instead of "Hello."

In the afternoon, the men of the town gathered on a cliff overlooking the sea to study the weather. If it seemed wise, they put out to sea after supper in their fishing-boats to fish by moonlight.

"The world," thought Lou, "is full of a number of things. Why is it, I wonder, that I can't like everything in it?"

During his stay at Wick he bribed an old diver to let him go down in a diver's suit. What a thrilling adventure that was. First twenty pounds of lead were strapped to each foot. Then he was wrapped up thickly in woolen clothing with a nightcap on his head. Then the heavy diver's helmet with the little window was set on his shoulders. Air whistled into this helmet through an air tube.

He could hear nothing; only motion to the men outside that he was ready. Someone put a rope in his hand. He lifted one heavy foot, then the other, and began slowly to climb down the ladder to the unfinished foundation of the breakwater below.

The moment he stepped off the ladder, of course, under the green water, he became light as a bubble. One skip sent him floating forward. Fish swam around him; he tried to catch them with his hands. There was no sound in the world at all.

But up in the air again, the gulls screamed monotonously, the sea pounded on the shore, the air smelled of fish and decayed seaweed. How he wished his mother would send him a basket of fruit and jelly.

The second summer after he went to the University Louis made a tour of the northern islands, the Orkneys and Shetlands, on the steam yacht belonging to the Board of Northern Lights. The summer that he was nineteen he toured the islands west of Scotland, especially one bare rocky island, called Earraid. Near Earraid there was a dangerous reef, where a lighthouse was being built. The island itself was covered with seaweed and shellfish. Some of the natives ate this shellfish raw, claiming that it was delicious. Others said that it made men deathly sick.

Louis himself did not try the shellfish. It was only later in his life, in the South Sea Islands, as a happy author, that he ventured cheerfully upon new food of all varieties. At this time he was much too bored with his occupation to have much spirit of adventure.

And yet his sharp eyes took in everything that was picturesque or unusual about the island. Years later, in the story of *Kidnapped,* he made Earraid the scene of David Balfour's shipwreck.

Chapter XVII

Now in the falling of the gloom
The red fire paints the empty room:
And warmly on the roof it looks
And flickers on the backs of books.

LOUIS' THIRD YEAR at the University was much happier.
In a more cheerful mood now, he went more often to
the meetings of the Speculative Society. These meetings
were held every Tuesday night in a great hall carpeted
in red and warmed by an open fire. Around the hall
hung portraits of famous members, lighted by candles.

After debating all evening, most of the members went
home. The rest stayed to talk further and drink watery
coffee made by old "Clues," the janitor. Louis always
stayed. He liked the after-sessions better than the regular
meetings. He felt more at ease then, more fun-loving. His
odd brown face glowed with pleasure in the candle-
light.

As the year advanced, he became friendly with a

young man named Charles Baxter. Baxter was witty and full of fun. He made a joke out of their not having much money to spend. A long walk to Queensferry to the dirty inn there for a glass of beer was an afternoon's pleasure to him. He liked to see the sailors at Queensferry, with gay handkerchiefs around their necks and knives stuck in their boots. When the tide was out, they went down to the beach to gather a particular kind of weed, long and brown, which had a little bladder that crackled between the fingers.

The following winter, with three friends from the Speculative Society, Louis started a magazine called the *Edinburgh University Magazine*. Everyone worked hard on the first number, which was published in January and sold for sixpence a copy. Louis wrote one article for the first number, two for the second, one for March, two for April. In one of these he wrote about umbrellas, the dear familiar umbrellas which had bobbed on the streets ever since he could remember. In another he wrote about the old gardener at Swanston, who quoted the Bible so aptly.

For four months the four friends kept the magazine alive, although the printer complained that they did not sell enough copies to pay their bills.

Meanwhile Louis was having another absorbing experience. Secretly, that winter, he became acquainted with a girl in the slums, whom he came to love dearly. This girl was simple and uneducated. He did not dare introduce her to his family and friends. But more often than anyone knew he was with her, and through her he came to pity more and more the cold, hungry people of the slums.

The effect of this love on him was to make him hate more and more the formal society to which his family and friends belonged. The people whom the girl knew called him "Velvet Coat" because of the dingy velvet lounging jacket he wore so often. Very well, he would wear that coat constantly, with a flannel shirt and tweed trousers and a cocked hat like Napoleon's. Formal dinner parties he now called "Noah's Ark" parties. He would not go to them. These things made his father very angry.

More serious still was his growing dislike for the profession of engineering. This feeling was soon to reach a crisis. Louis knew and liked the engineering professor, Dr. Jenkin, but he avoided his house, his classes. Tucked away in the brown notebook, which he carried always with him, were many doggerel verses about long-faced engineers.

In March of that year, when he was twenty years old, he read a paper on *A New Form of Intermittent Light for Lighthouses* before the Royal Scottish Society of Arts. The paper was highly praised; he received a silver medal for it. But the sight of all those engineers at the meeting made his heart go down into his boots. He wanted to be a *writer,* not an engineer in a silk hat and a frock coat. Ten days later he told his father flatly, plainly, that he would not be an engineer.

The scene with his father was very painful to both of them. It took place while they were walking out to Cramond, a suburb by the sea, with a great stretch of quicksand in front of it.

"I can no' be an engineer, father," said Louis abruptly.

"Ye can no' be an engineer! Of course ye can be an engineer! Why, your father and grandfather and his father before him——"

"Ay, ay, father, I ken. But I can no' be one."

Mr. Stevenson became excited, angry.

"Are ye daft, laddie? Whammling at the engineering! (By "whammling" he meant shrinking from.) Ye've been running about wi' riffraff till ye are an idle, lazy fellow. Ye've a man's work to do in the wurrld."

"Yes, father, but I wish to be a writer."

"A writer is it! Well, I *am* gravelled (stumped). I'll have no writers in my family."

"But, father, I like writing. I have always liked it."

"Hardly a man's work," said Mr. Stevenson positively.

"I can work at that, father. I do work at it."

"I said hardly a man's work," said Mr. Stevenson harshly. "Let us say no more about it."

A few days later, seeing his father's deep despair,

93

Louis suggested that he might read for the bar, instead of writing, by which he meant he might study law. A new friend of his, Walter Simpson, was studying law. Walter talked a great deal about how difficult it was for a young lawyer to get cases. Sometimes, he said, they waited years after graduation before someone hired them to do some legal work. Hearing him say this, Lou sat staring into the fire for several minutes. Perhaps this very thing might happen to him! In that case he would have plenty of free time in which to write!

Mr. Stevenson looked a little more pleased when Louis suggested that he was willing to read for the bar. Perhaps after all the boy had no taste for engineering. He had been a delicate lad from the beginning. After thinking it over for several days he told Louis to go ahead with the new program, never dreaming that, in his heart, Louis still intended to be a writer.

Chapter XVIII

My bonny man, the world it's true,
Was made for neither me nor you;
It's just a place to warstle through.
As Job confessed o' it.

THE FALL CAME, and Louis returned to the University, to study Civil Law, Public Law, and Politics.

That winter he saw more and more of Walter Simpson. Walter lived with his brother and sister in a house on the other side of Queen Street Gardens in Queen Street itself. Lou went there often, to dine, for late supper, to sit up in the night and talk.

And how Louis could talk. So fast and so much, sometimes, that the butler, Jarvis, had to "shuggle" his elbow at dinner to get him to notice the potatoes he was offering! The butler said young Mr. Stevenson had a "skilpit" look, which meant that he looked half-starved and neglected.

How Cummy would have raged at the idea that any-one thought her boy looked neglected. Nothing, apparently, would make him grow any fatter. The clothes, which she herself mended and pressed, hung in his closet, while he continued to wear the oldest and worst garments he owned. She could no longer tell him what he should wear, as she had done in the old days. Now that Louis was grown, Cummy had become Mrs. Stevenson's companion and general helper.

Meanwhile Louis was very happy being informal with the Simpsons, who liked him very much. One night when the cook and butler were out they gave a dinner party. Louis came in evening clothes to act as waiter. First, he made himself a cap and apron of newspaper. Then he put two round red cheeses on the side board, carved grinning faces on them, and arranged stalks of celery for hair.

The guests sat down. Louis dealt out the silver like a deck of cards. The guests must eat with whatever pieces they received. As the soiled plates accumulated, the "waiter" pushed them under the table. How his laughter rang out; how many witty remarks he made!

Why couldn't he be happy and charming like this at a sensible dinner party? That is hard to say. But no one could doubt that he was very happy and very charming when he was at the Simpsons' house.

In the evening at home the family dined formally at

six o'clock. Afterward Lou smoked a cigar with his father in the library. Then he worked upstairs in the old nursery, now his study, until about nine o'clock. At that hour a cold supper was served downstairs. Lou, however, rarely staying to eat it. Over at the Simpsons' conversation was raging. By rattling with a key on the iron letter-box, he could get in, even though the servants were in bed when he arrived. Almost any hour of the night he was sure of a warm welcome.

In cheerful companionship of this kind much of the year 1872 passed.

In February Louis was elected one of the five vice-presidents of the Speculative Society. In March and April he went to Brussels with his parents. In May he worked for two months in a law office, and this dampened his spirits a little, but he was able to shake off his depression as soon as the office door closed behind him at night, for he promptly forgot about the law.

Bob was at home now, and the two rambled together. Seeing a beggar-boy asleep on a park bench one day, they put a penny in his pocket. Lou laughed to think how the beggar-boy would rub his head, wondering how the penny got in his pocket.

Summer brought Swanston again. Out under the trees he read Walt Whitman, the sturdy American poet. Walt was full of courage and cheerful philosophy. He made Louis think that one must be strong and brave and gracious. If a man lost heart for a little while, he must somehow find it again without complaining.

In July and August he went to Germany with Walter Simpson, and sat out under the trees at a café, eating bread and cheese and sausages, listening to the German bands. At night the famous German clocks chimed at all hours, not all together, as they were supposed to do. This made Louis laugh.

He found he liked to travel. He wished he could travel more. Inwardly he chafed at the small amount of money he had to spend, when his father could afford to give him much more if only he would. Inwardly, too, he still liked ordinary people best, still visited the girl in the back street, although not so often now.

At home his father eyed him with a good deal of disapproval. He could not understand his son's liking for poor, shabby people, his refusal to go to formal parties. Also Louis' clothes distressed him. The other young men he knew wore gloves and a silk hat above the most conventional garments.

Worst of all, perhaps, Mr. Stevenson suspected that Louis was forming religious beliefs different from his own. Such a thought was terrible to him. He began to ask the boy questions about what he thought and did. The more questions he asked the more critical he became. A great chill sprang up between them, which made Louis avoid his father's presence.

Seeking the pleasantest things he knew, he spent a great deal of time at the "Spec," at his writing, and with his books, during that winter when he was twenty-three. And when the end of the school year came, he put his knapsack on his back and went for a walk in England.

What a memorable trip that proved to be. With nothing but his knapsack he went all the way down the east coast of England till he came to the county of Suffolk, not so far north of London. Near Cockfield in this county one of his cousins lived. Louis dropped in on her one evening, and liked it so well that he stayed nearly a month.

The reason why he liked Cockfield was not hard to find. There was a lady staying at Cockfield, a lovely, gentle lady named Mrs. Sitwell, eight years older than Louis. To her he opened up his heart.

He explained that he loved uncommon adventure, that he wished to write, that he was sometimes happy and then again very, very sad.

"Yes," said Mrs. Sitwell, "but you must harness your feelings. If you wish to write you must work patiently at it, finish a story or essay, and send it off to an editor for consideration. You dream too much, do too little, hate the law and your father's disapproval, but do not work at what you do like."

99

"That is true," said Louis.

They were walking in the fields near Cockfield. Mrs. Sitwell seemed to him like a lamp in a dark room.

Mrs. Sitwell had a friend in London, Mr. Sidney Colvin, who knew magazine editors and publishers. She wrote to him about this brown, thin Scotchman with the burning eyes and the cough.

"What are you reading; what are you thinking now?" asked Mrs. Sitwell the next afternoon.

"I am thinking about roads," answered Louis. "Roads are romantic. They take you somewhere. I remember sitting on the London Road as a child, and crying over a cat."

"You must write an essay on roads—a serious essay," she said.

So Louis worked in his room the next morning, and felt that she was right about everything.

Sidney Colvin came up from London for the weekend, and met Louis Stevenson. He liked him. Louis talked to him and Mrs. Sitwell about Walt Whitman.

"He was a great man," he said. "He had courage to be himself, to do what he wanted most to do."

"You must write an essay on Walt Whitman," said Mrs. Sitwell.

Louis went home to Edinburgh with fire in his heart.

But trouble was brewing for him at home. Mr. Stevenson welcomed him with a long face. He had heard further stories about Louis' change of religious feeling. In a series of stormy scenes he blamed Bob, dear cousin Bob, for this change of feeling. Bob, he said, could no longer come to the house.

The effect of these scenes on Louis' nerves was disastrous. He could not sleep, nor eat, nor work. Instead of writing the article on Walt Whitman, he could only sit in his room writing frantic letters to Mrs. Sitwell in London, telling her his trouble. Mrs. Sitwell suggested that he come down to see Sidney Colvin, perhaps try to study law in London instead of Edinburgh.

Louis went, but his stay in London was brief. Almost as soon as he arrived, he became very ill. A doctor was called in, his mother came down, white-faced, from Edinburgh. The doctor said that Louis was suffering from a nervous breakdown, that he must go away somewhere for a long rest.

Chapter XIX

Thus on my pipe I breathed a strain or two;
It scarce was music, but 'twas all I knew.
It was not music, for I lacked the art,
Yet what but frozen music filled my heart?

IN THE SOUTH of France there was peace and quiet for
the nervous Louis for five months. In Mentone the sun
was shining. There was a smell of lemons and oranges
in the air. At the hotel two pretty Russian ladies made
friends with him, there was a French painter to talk to,
an American family whom he liked.

Sitting all day by the sea he grew better and began to
write again, the essay on Walt Whitman. Good news
came from London: a magazine called *The Portfolio*
would publish his essay on *Roads*. This was his first
published essay. How proud that made him feel.

In December Sidney Colvin came for a few weeks, and
together they marveled at the blooming violets. Colvin
went up to Paris, and sent him down a great blue cape,
immensely warm, with a buckle like a silver snake at the

neck. At night now he burned two candles down to the saucer, and did not feel tired or sick at all. He finished the essay on Walt Whitman, and began another one about his trip called *Ordered South*. France was indeed a magic country!

In April he went up to Paris to spend a few weeks with Bob, who came over from Holland to meet him. Together they made a kind of picnic out of Paris, as Bob made a picnic out of everything.

And so Louis came home to Edinburgh, calmer, a better writer, brown and comparatively healthy, with a new golden moustache that was very becoming. His father made things much easier for him now by increasing his allowance to seven pounds (thirty-five dollars) a month. This made it possible for him to do the things he liked with his friends, without being embarrassed for money. With money in his pocket, he could travel a good deal in his free time. From that year Louis was an incurable, an extravagant traveler to the day of his death.

In June he went to London to visit Sidney Colvin, and joined a men's club there—the Savile Club, where all the members talked to each other as friends, whether they were acquainted or not. In July he went yachting with Walter Simpson off the west coast of Scotland, and thumbed his nose at all the harbor works he saw. In August he went to Wales, a mountainous country west of England, full of rushing rivers.

Winter came, and he must study law again. This was his last year. Examinations lay ahead the next July. But other things interested him more. There was his writing: how he worked at that now. He knew that one must work and plan, not dream and drift. Life was like that. Courage must come every morning.

In November he was back in London with Sidney Colvin and Mrs. Sitwell. He was much in love with Mrs. Sitwell these days, although he knew he could not marry her. To see her and be with her, however, always brought him fresh courage. With her he visited the British Museum and saw the Elgin marbles, the most beautiful Greek carving in the world. Louis found them so beautiful that he felt himself melting inside as he looked at them. Before leaving the museum he bought some photographs of the marbles.

Sidney Colvin, too, gave him some pictures, Japanese prints, for his study back home. One of these showed a red king on a white horse against a background of blue sea. No wonder Louis, who had colored so many pictures on his nursery floor as a child, loved these pictures. No wonder Edinburgh seemed cold and dreary when he got back with them and hung them on his study wall.

In spite of this, however, he wrote several articles during the winter, and was cheerful much of the time. One reason why he was cheerful was because he had made a new friend. The new friend was a patient in a charity hospital in Edinburgh, a large, lively, red-bearded man, who was a poet. The poet's name was William Henley. He had been in the hospital a year and a half, and had lost one of his legs, yet he remained cheerful and full of fun. For many years he and Louis Stevenson were friends.

When spring came, and Louis had several weeks of vacation, there seemed but one sensible thing for him to do—go back to France, where Bob was, and feel again the warmth of France.

Bob was staying now in the little village of Barbizon, twelve miles from Paris, on the edge of a great forest called Fontainebleau. Millet, the famous French painter, had lived at Barbizon. He was only just dead. The fields that he painted, the peasant-farmers in their blue smocks, the great plumey poplar trees along the highways, were still there for eager young art students to paint. The forest of Fontainebleau—quiet, cool, green, full of big gray rocks—lay up the road from the inn where most of the students lived.

Bob met Louis in Paris, and together they drove down to Barbizon in the stagecoach, arriving one evening about six o'clock. The students welcomed Bob noisily. He was a great favorite among them; they called him "Talking Bob."

At first the young painters did not pay much attention to Bob's cousin, the thin, elongated Louis with the nervous white hands and brilliant brown eyes. They merely dragged him along with Bob into the billiard room for a glass of wine before they all filed in to the dining room for dinner. Mr. Siron, who ran the inn, brought in the soup with a great flourish. "To the table, Sirs!" he cried, setting the big dish on the table. The boys broke pieces of bread into their soup after the French fashion.

While he was eating, Louis looked around him. The dining room was long and narrow, lit by candles and lamps. All around the walls were pictures: good pictures, bad pictures, any old pictures, pictures of trees, of wild boars, of fish, fruit, peasants, gardens, bridges. In a corner some one was playing on a crazy piano.

The students who ate at Siron's did not all sleep there. Some of them lived in the peasants' houses up and down the village street. The courtyard outside the dining room was filled with painters' materials. Everyone at the table was talking about painting. It was a world of art and artists.

The word-painter, Louis, loved them all. After dinner he went out happily for a walk by moonlight through the forest. To reach the forest one had only to walk up the village street a little way until it became a mere lane, called the "Alley of the Cows."

In the morning the cooing of doves under the eaves awakened him. When he went downstairs, he found everyone drinking coffee or cold milk hastily out of bowls, before setting off to paint. Some painted in the forest; some in the open fields; some in the village itself, or in near-by villages.

Bob was there, ready to paint, with a blue cap on the side of his head, a blue jersey, paint-splashed trousers and wooden peasant-shoes. Apparently, in this happy-go-lucky place, Louis' taste for loose, shabby clothes would not even be noticed! How nice it was to be in a place where he could be comfortable.

Louis was not well that morning, or for several days, but later in the week he was able to go out with Bob. While Bob painted, Louis sat on a knoll with his note-book, watching the yellow butterflies and planning some writing.

These happy days lasted several weeks. Then Louis must go reluctantly home to read law again, although he spent his week-ends at Swanston with his parents or his friends. Spring was slow in coming to Swanston that year. The trees dripped with spring rain, the mist clung to them, as Louis said, "like wet cotton." Still he heard the love songs of the blackbirds, saw baby rabbits on his walks over the hills.

One thing he did that pleased his father. He wrote an article on the Scotch poet, Robert Burns, for the *Encyclopaedia Britannica.* Then he wrote an essay, called *Forest Notes,* about Fontainebleau where he had stayed in France. In this essay there were some very charming descriptions of the forest, of Siron's Inn, of the young painters eating and talking at dinner. This essay was perhaps the first thing he wrote that showed his great talent for descriptive writing. Later on he wrote many remarkably good travel essays and books.

His examinations as a lawyer came early in July. In Scotland they called this being "called to the bar." By the fifteenth of July, he knew that he was successful, and wrote jubilantly to Mrs. Sitwell in London to tell her about it.

Chapter XX

On the great streams the ships may go
About men's business to and fro.
But I, the egg-shell pinnace, sleep
On crystal waters ankle-deep.

SO A BURNING young writer, not quite twenty-five, who
didn't care much for the law, could still pass the
examinations and qualify as a lawyer. What a queer thing
that was.

The rest of the summer Louis spent at Barbizon, resting
from the strain of his examinations. By November, however, he was back in gray, rainy Edinburgh, ready to begin
his work. This meant that every day he must put on his
lawyer's black gown and gray wig, and go to the law
courts in Parliament Square to listen to cases being tried.
Seeing him there, men in need of his services would
gradually bring him other cases; that was the way a law
practice usually developed.

But the cases Louis heard revolted him. Poor, wretched

men being tried for murder, sheep-stealing, unpaid debts. In their faces one could see that they were often hungry and helpless—neglected, dirty children from the slums grown up into violent, miserable men. The business of punishing them for their misdeeds seemed to him sordid and dreadful.

And so Louis was once more the unhappy rebel, dreaming of a life that would fit his own tastes, without being able to find it. What a disappointment it all was. How ridiculous his black gown and gray wig seemed to him. If his long brown hair—longer than most men's—hung down below his wig, making him look untidy, what did it matter? Would he ever be able to do the things that seemed important to him?

Thinking these thoughts, he buried himself for hours daily in the great library for lawyers, and read books on every other subject but law. Most of them were about great soldiers or writers in the past. How he loved the maps of Scotland that told of this battle and that. Or the lives of great writers—Goethe, Victor Hugo, Dumas. Here were men who struggled to be what they wanted to be.

The winter was long and wretched for Louis. In his despondency, he saw a good deal of Walter Simpson. And here was a puzzle. Simpson, whom he liked, was a lawyer, too, and liked it! There was nothing painful to Simpson about his work. Digging out rules of law, wait-

110

ing for cases, walking neatly up and down Parliament Square were to him satisfying and interesting experiences.

"The world," thought Louis, "is full of a number of things—riddles mostly!"

Despairing of solving these riddles, he turned at night to pleasant planning. Wrapping himself in his blue cape, and putting on a Spanish fez, like a pirate, he went to visit Simpson in order to plan a canoe-trip they were hoping to take the following summer.

The trip was made in August, 1876, the summer before he was twenty-six, and was a great success. Their plan was to sail two canoes down the canal from Antwerp, Holland, to Brussels, Belgium, and then, taking the canoe by train into France, sail down the River Oise to Grez, a little town near Barbizon. Each man carried his dry clothes in a long rubber bag.

The first few days it rained, which gave them a doubtful feeling. Sitting in a ditch for luncheon the second day, with water streaming from their eggs and bread and wine, they wondered if they were really going to have a good time. But eventually the sun came out, the sails puffed out before them, and they were able to spend long, lazy days floating gently downstream. At Brussels they followed their plan of taking a train into France to the River Oise.

The people along the bank of the river were amazed at them. No one had ever sailed a canoe in that part of

France before. Fishermen put down their poles to watch them. Children spat at them over bridges. Families living in barges along the river bank scrambled ashore and followed them on their way. When they landed near an inn, people came down to the water-side and fingered the canoes. One man got up early to see them off, and breakfasted with them in the inn coffee-room on white wine and raw onions!

Presently, however, the river grew wider, the current swifter. They must paddle now for their lives in some places. At one place the low branch of a tree lifted Louis clear out of his canoe, and left him hanging perilously, clinging to his paddle, while the canoe rode on downstream. With great difficulty he was rescued.

"Anyhow I hung on to my paddle, if I did lose the canoe," he said proudly to Simpson afterward. "When I die you can print this on my tombstone.

'HE CLUNG TO HIS PADDLE.' "

"Don't be foolish," said Walter severely. "It was a very dangerous experience. Next time watch out for branches."

The wetting which Louis received that day made his throat sore. For the rest of the trip he complained about it. But his face was burned a bright red, and he looked strong and healthy when they landed at Grez one evening and went up the garden to the inn for supper.

The inn at Grez, like the inn at Barbizon, was full of

art students. Louis had been there before. He knew that it was kept by Madame Chevillon, an old woman with a wrinkled brown face and sharp eyes.

Grez itself was more out in the open country than Barbizon. It had a greater variety of things to paint: a mill, a church, a ruined castle, an old stone bridge, sheep wandering in the village street. Then there was the river at the foot of the inn garden, where the students might bathe or paddle canoes in the evening. The meals at Chevillon's were served out in the garden overlooking the river. For all these reasons, many of the students preferred Grez to Barbizon.

Louis himself had never felt that way, because of his great love for the forest. But that evening in August his feeling underwent a remarkable change. Suddenly, romantically, he fell in love with a lady at Grez.

The lady was Mrs. Fanny Osbourne, an American woman, brown-skinned, with a kind of gypsy beauty and a red ribbon in her hair. She was older than Louis. He was twenty-five, while she was thirty-six. But Louis had always liked older, wiser women than himself.

Mrs. Osbourne had two children: Lloyd, a boy of eight, and Isabel, a girl old enough to study painting. Both the mother and daughter had come all the way from America to study painting at Grez.

The boy, Lloyd, liked Louis instantly. This tall, brown man in the flannel shirt and schoolboy cap looked like a good playmate. So he was, for after supper Louis took Lloyd down to see his canoe, and showed him how to make the sails go up and down.

When the boy was in bed, however, his mother and Louis sat in the garden on a stone bench talking. She asked him about his trip, said she envied him such an adventure. Louis declared enthusiastically that it was the kind of thing he loved best to do, that he would rather "die in a ditch" than live the life of cities and offices.

Mrs. Osbourne said she had some Spanish blood in her, that she loved adventure, too.

"Then we must walk and talk together," cried Louis. "For my taste is all for that."

After that he carried her paint boxes and brushes out for her every day, and sat by her side while she painted. When it got too cold to sit longer in the garden evenings, they sat beside the stove in the inn dining room, and talked far into the night.

Sometimes Louis was ill and peevish, for his throat did not seem to get quite well. At such times Mrs. Osbourne came up to his room, bringing hot things to drink. Soon he was downstairs again, sitting talking by the stove.

This was all very well, but what could come of this romance? Mrs. Osbourne was a married woman separated from her husband. She had two children to be educated. Louis was a young lawyer, running away from the practice

114

of law and dependent on his father for his living, while he wrote essays for the magazines.

When these facts became suddenly clear to him about the first of October, he packed up in some haste and went home to Edinburgh. A new year at the bar was waiting for him there with the opening of the fall sessions of court. Certainly his father still expected him to take hold of the law with a good heart. As for Louis himself his determination to write was as firmly fixed as ever, and now there was this new distraction to draw his thoughts away from Edinburgh.

Chapter XXI

I will make you brooches and toys for your delight
Of bird-song at morning and star-shine at night.
I will make a palace fit for you and me
Of green days in forests and blue days at sea.

LOUIS DID NOT remain long in Edinburgh. The same chill
in the air, the same uneasiness with his father, took hold
of him again once he was back. In January he made ex-
cuses to get away, and went down to London to see
Colvin and his other friends at the Savile Club. Colvin
introduced him to a man named Edmund Gosse, a critic
of books.

Gosse saw that Louis was like quicksilver, restless and
active. He delighted in Louis' way of talking. He
marveled at the fact that he never sat properly on a chair,
but roosted here and there, now on a footstool, now on
the floor, now on the window sill, all the time talking and
emphasizing what he said with his hands.

"I hate chairs!" said Louis. "Stuffy, boring people sit on chairs."

"Not everyone," said Gosse, "is as alive as you are, as full of imagination and feeling. People need to rest sometimes."

"Not I," said Louis. "When I am tired I go to bed. Even beds are not essential. I would rather die in a ditch than in a bed in any case."

Gosse loved this quick, active artist, this strenuous Louis, whom so many people loved, Colvin, Simpson, Baxter, Bob, and Fanny Osbourne.

Meanwhile Colvin was not idle in helping Louis. He had written again to Louis' father, telling him how gifted he thought the young man was, how surely he must be a writer, not a lawyer. Colvin was now Keeper of Prints at the British Museum. His word had weight. Influenced somewhat by Colvin's letters, and by his own shrewd observation of his son, Mr. Stevenson decided to let Louis go his own way at last.

His first generous step in that direction was to give Louis a nest egg of a thousand pounds (five thousand dollars). Alas, it was an egg which did not stay long in the nest. Cheerfully, all too rapidly, Louis spent the money on himself and his friends in less than two years.

His first move was to go to France where Bob and Fanny were. There he remained during February, again in June and July, finally from August to November. And there he began to write with great zeal, more steadily and quietly than ever before. The story of his canoe trip became a charming little travel book, called *An Inland Voyage.* He began also to write stories, breaking away from the essays he had written before.

By the end of the year he was buzzing with things he wished to write. Henley had come down to London, out of the hospital at last, hobbling cheerfully on crutches. There, he was editing a magazine. Louis began a series of stories for this magazine, called *New Arabian Nights.* These first stories were grim and a little awful in some ways, but they described people cleverly, too.

Louis also wrote for Henley's magazine some very moving chapters of a little book to be called *Picturesque Notes on Edinburgh.* How he enjoyed writing that book, tucked away in Paris as he was. For though he now turned his back on Edinburgh for months at a time, Louis was Scottish to the bone. The memory of Edinburgh as he had seen it as a child, as a schoolboy, as a young man, thrilled him still.

His room in Paris was in the students' quarters of the city. Old buildings, crooked streets, simple people were around him. The students made themselves at home in attics, courtyards, humble restaurants. Very often there were birdcages in the windows of these dark and dingy rooms.

In his own room Louis had a cage of tiny birds, little

golden fellows no bigger than his thumb, who sat on his table while he worked and sang, as he said, "like bees in a garden." Sitting thus with his birds, he wrote about the gray, rainy city of Edinburgh.

That summer in Paris, Louis also acted as secretary to his old engineering professor from Edinburgh, who was there in charge of the International Exhibit. This work interrupted his writing, but it kept him in Paris, with friends, near Fanny. For, in a foolish, far-away fashion, Fanny and Louis talked sometimes of being married, planned a life of adventure together, revelled in gypsy tastes.

A marriage between them was impossible. Yet still they dreamed of somehow being united, two people against the world. Meanwhile Fanny's money was giving out. In August, 1878, she could postpone the day no longer, and set sail from London for San Francisco with her children.

Left behind in Paris, Louis was rebellious, but still he finished his work with Professor Jenkin. Then he retired to the little town of Monastier in the mountains, and worked furiously for three weeks to finish the two books on which he was working, the *New Arabian Nights* and the *Picturesque Notes on Edinburgh*. If he could not marry and support his loved ones, he could write like a tormented spirit, and did. The knowledge of his loss lent wings to his pencil.

Meanwhile, he was making preparations for a solitary tramp through the mountains to clear his head of pain and work. These preparations were elaborate. First he bought a small gray donkey, then a revolver, a lantern, a jack-knife, cans of sausages, etc., as well as having a sleeping bag made, according to specifications. This sleeping bag was lined with blue sheep's-wool, for the nights would be cold. The donkey, who was small, mouse-colored, and determined, was to be his only companion. Everyone in the village thought he was crazy to make such a trip.

When it came time to depart, his appearance was ludicrous. The donkey could not carry all the baggage. Louis himself stood in the road with a basket containing the extra things—bottles of wine, a cold leg of mutton, black bread for the donkey, white bread for himself, an extra coat. Before they were many feet up the road, the donkey's share of the load slid exasperatingly from his back down under his belly! Nevertheless, they made a fresh start, and got under way successfully at last.

Louis' plan was to climb up over several rocky ridges, camping out if he must, or sleeping in tiny inns. This plan he carried out successfully. For two days he stayed in a monastery on a mountain, and shared the life of the monks in the high, cold atmosphere. Once he had only chocolate and cold sausage for supper in a wood, while the wolves howled near by. But at the end of two weeks he had walked one hundred and twenty miles, and felt sparkling with health and new vigor.

Fanny, apparently, he must, he could forget.

But could he? Returning to Edinburgh he wrote the story of his trip, *Travels With a Donkey*, an amusing and charming tale. Then he went to London and began to write a play with Henley on the old story of Deacon Brodie, the cabinet-maker by day, the burglar by night. From London he went back to Swanston, from Swanston to London, from London up to Swanston and back, and finally to France in May.

All this running back and forth was not necessary to his work. It showed instead the agitated state of his mind. For Fanny was writing from California that she could not forget him, that she could get a divorce, that the gypsy marriage might some day take place. Louis, in his turn, longed to go to her, but could not see how he could support her and her children by his writing, which had never paid more than a few hundred dollars a year.

One thing was clear, and that was that he must support them if he went. Taking money from his father had always been painful. Now that he had spent his nest egg so recklessly, it would be impossible to ask his father for money for himself and three other people. If he was to marry Fanny at all, he must find some way to make a living.

Meanwhile, Fanny felt sick, and wrote him again. Suddenly he made up his mind. Gathering together what money he could, much too little money, he decided to start for America. In the middle of July he went up to Edinburgh to see his parents, without ever telling them of his decision. Then he came down to London to say goodbye to his friends.

Colvin begged him not to go. Gosse argued with him. In the end he turned his back on them all, and sailed from Glasgow on the seventh of August without even saying goodbye to his family.

Penny Whistles

Chapter XXII

Home no more home to me,
Whither must I wander?
Hunger my driver,
I go where I must.

THE TRIP TO America was full of interest and hardship. Louis traveled second class on the boat. This meant that he did not have a good stateroom, in fact it was so hot and stuffy that he slept the eleven nights of the voyage in a blanket on the deck. The food also was not very good. All the way over he ate chiefly oatmeal or soup and bread for his meals.

Arriving in New York in a drenching rain, he rode to his hotel in an open wagon. The hotel was really a cheap Irish boarding-house. When he got there he found that he must still sleep on the floor, since the bed they offered him was not wide enough for two, and he had a friend from the boat with him.

In the morning it was still raining, such rain as never

fell in Edinburgh. All day Louis traveled about the city, making arrangements to start for California that night in an immigrant train. How unusual these experiences were for the frail, lovable Louis, brought up in a wealthy home.

The journey to California was very disagreeable. The immigrant train traveled slowly. It had no upholstered seats, only wooden benches. Food was available only at the stations, where they sold it alongside in a hurried, careless fashion. For days Louis was never nimble enough, or rude enough, to get a cup of coffee before the urn was empty. Babies cried. There were no berths at all, only a board and three cushions laid across two seats at night for two persons to lie on.

In his bag Louis carried a history of the United States in six volumes. After several days of travel, however, he was too tired to read, merely sat staring out at the fields of wheat and corn, the mountains, rivers, and empty deserts. Altogether, it took eleven and a half days to reach San Francisco.

When he arrived, he traveled another hundred and fifty miles south to the town of Monterey, California. Fanny Osbourne was at Monterey; that was why he went there. But having reached the town he rode up into the mountains on horseback to camp out. The reason why he decided to camp out was that he hesitated to spend the money for a room and meals in Monterey. Apparently he was never again to get into a bed and sleep like other men.

The camping-out at the end of his trip proved disastrous. By the time Louis reached camp and lay down beside his horse he was so ill and feverish with malaria that he scarcely got up at all for two days. Once or twice he staggered up to give his horse a pail of water, and then lay down again and lost himself before his own coffee had boiled.

If two men from a near-by goat-ranch had not found him on the second day, he might have died up there. As it was, they carried him down to the goat-ranch, and put him to bed in a bunk that seemed like heaven after his experiences of the past weeks. Here he stayed, amazed at their rough kindness, for two weeks, recovering strength enough to go down to Monterey again.

Monterey, at that time, was more Mexican than American. It consisted merely of a street or two of adobe houses, lying on a hook of land out in the Pacific Ocean. Surf and salt beaches lay on both sides of it. The streets themselves were paved with sea sand instead of stones, although behind the houses there were pretty gardens.

Here in this new-world town Louis stayed for three months, cut off from his family and friends, writing feverishly, not at all well, and living in the most haphazard fashion. One meal a day he took in a sailors' restaurant. The others he ate in his cheap room. Part of his expenses he earned by writing at two dollars a week for a local paper. With his delicate constitution, it was a dangerous way for him to live.

His courage, however, did not weaken during this period. Louis was gay, whimsical, cheerful. Every afternoon he and Lloyd walked on the beach, playing that they were Indians, pirates, naval officers. When the fashionable men of Monterey rode by, they admired their silver-topped saddles and bridles worth hundreds of dollars. Together they discussed how it would feel to be so prosperous.

Meanwhile, prosperity seemed far away, for his work was not going well. Two or three essays and a long story were accepted in England, but longer, more profitable manuscripts gave him trouble. One of these, a travel book describing his journey out, seemed dismal to Colvin. Half of a novel, over which he worked very hard, did not please him. Another novel, to be called *Prince Otto,* was still unfinished when he fell ill in December with pleurisy, and had to stop all work for several weeks.

Recovering a little, he went up to San Francisco. Here his health broke down completely. The old tuberculosis, which had been hanging over him since he was a child, broke out actively. At first he was merely weak and feverish. Then a great heaviness came over him. Finally blood came up into his mouth from his lungs, a sure sign of the disease he dreaded.

Lonely and far away from home, Louis considered what this might mean to him. Most people, he knew, did not recover from tuberculosis. Well, then, he would be brave and gay, and go cheerfully.

Buoyed up by this resolve, he took out his old brown notebook and wrote in it eight beautiful lines of poetry. This is what he wrote:

> "Under the wide and starry sky,
> Dig the grave and let me die.
> Glad did I live and gladly die,
> And I laid me down with a will.
>
> This be the verse you grave for me;
> *Here he lies where he longed to be;*
> *Home is the sailor, home from the sea,*
> *And the hunter home from the hill."*

Here was the man Stevenson, sick and in great trouble, singing bravely. How different from the moody young man he had been in his student days. He was now strong enough to meet the worst fate cheerfully.

In the meantime, Fanny Osbourne was horrified at what had happened. Very firmly she made up her mind that Louis should not die. Moving nearer to him, she began to nurse him night and day. She also wrote several strong, forceful letters to his friends at home, telling them what had happened to Louis and that he must have money. She knew that Mr. Stevenson was a wealthy man who loved his son dearly. How ridiculous that Louis should be here ill in America without his help.

The result of her efforts was that early in April there came a cablegram from Louis' father, sending money and an offer of more each week from then on.

Chapter XXIII

The thorn shall blow
In the month of May,
And my love shall go
In her holiday array.

THE AMOUNT WHICH Mr. Stevenson promised to send
Louis was twenty-five dollars a week. This was not a
large sum, not nearly large enough for a family of three
or four to live on. But in his reckless fashion, Louis made
plans immediately to marry Fanny Osbourne. On the
nineteenth of May, in that year 1880, when he was
twenty-nine, they were married quietly at a minister's
house.

A few days later they went up into the mountains
north of San Francisco in search of health. Louis was,
as he said afterward, "a mere complication of coughs
and bones."

The stagecoach took them as far as a decayed ranch on
the side of the mountain. From there they scrambled up

a mountain trail on foot, till they came to the mouth of an abandoned silver mine, called Juan Silverado. A cluster of shacks opening on a wooden platform stood at the mouth of this mine. It was here they meant to camp until Louis' lungs were better.

The shacks and the platform were not in very good condition. Flowers and weeds grew up between the planks, looked in at the windows. The bunk-house was full of old lumber. Nevertheless, there was a delicious piney smell in the air, and the water in the well was clear and sparkling. In a few days they were settled comfortably enough, with a stove and a few chairs, cooking pots and provisions.

Here for two months Louis lived out in the open on the platform, while his lungs healed in the mountain air.

Meanwhile, every mail brought more letters from his father and mother, begging him to come home. In the end he went, sailing from New York on the seventh of August, exactly one year after he sailed from Glasgow. But with him on the return trip were his new wife and the boy, Lloyd, or Sam, as they sometimes called him.

His father and mother and Sidney Colvin met them at Liverpool. There were tears in Mrs. Stevenson's eyes as she kissed her son. Mr. Stevenson looked at the new wife critically, and decided that she looked sensible.

From Liverpool the family went north for a month's

132

stay in the Highland country on the west coast of Scotland. No sooner was Louis there than he began to study Highland history. Like all Scotch history, he found it full of exciting incidents.

A month later they all went home to Edinburgh for Louis to be examined by the doctor. The doctor, who was also his Uncle George, said Louis must go to Switzerland for the winter.

Walter Simpson came with a present of a black Skye terrier, named Woggs, who was to go with them. Mr. Stevenson arranged to send them money and books from time to time. The boy, Lloyd, packed up his toy printing-press and his box of paints. And so they set out for Davos in Switzerland, a little straggling town in the high Alps, where tubercular patients went to get the winter sunshine.

That first winter in Davos was disagreeable. Stevenson hated the idea of being in a health resort. The hotel where they stayed was full of sick people. Each week there was a public weighing-day for the invalids. Tonics, cod-liver oil, beef tea met him at every hand. What a life that was for a man who loved adventure.

Davos itself was beautiful, but monotonous. All around it towered the high Alps. One little rushing river fell through the town. Snow buried everything and everybody to the eye-brows. Louis, who must be out-of-doors as much as possible, walked and skated and tobogganed. Indoors he played with Woggs, or helped Lloyd to print or play soldiers.

Some days he was not even well enough for that, days when a heavy sleepiness came over him, "the limpness and lack of appetite peculiar to a kid glove," he said. And yet he chafed because in this condition he could not work. The best he could do was to write a short magazine article now and then. Since this was true, he was obliged to take money from his father for his expenses. How he hated being dependent on his father—a grown man, married, writing home for money like a schoolboy. The fact that he was ill did not seem excuse enough.

Meanwhile he read books on Highland history, collecting material for a great history of the Highlands he meant to write some day.

How glad he was to leave Davos in May, and go back to Edinburgh. From there the whole family went again to the Highlands for the summer. Their first stop was at Pitlochry, with a mountain, called in Scotland a "ben", up behind the cottage. Here Louis wrote two stories of Scotch life—*Thrawn Janet* and *The Merry Men,* both gruesome stories which he called "crawlers."

Fanny also wrote some "crawlers" that summer. In some ways Fanny was a strange woman. She loved supernatural, ghostly things. At times, too, she was impatient and angry. But she was also a strong, attractive woman. Louis loved her very dearly.

The weather at Pitlochry was wet and cold. In July they moved on to Braemar under another "ben." Still it rained and the fog clung to the trees. For days at a time they were all shut up in the house together, waiting for the clouds to lift. Again Louis became too ill to write anything. How restless and thwarted this made him feel.

In these idle days he looked back with longing to the days of his childhood, when he played on the lawn at Colinton. The thought of those precious days brought verses to his mind. In his old brown notebook he began to write them down.

One day he wrote,

> "When at home alone I sit
> And am very tired of it,
> I have just to shut my eyes
> To go sailing through the skies—
> To go sailing far away
> To the pleasant Land of Play
> To the fairy land afar
> Where the Little People are;
> Where the clover-tops are trees,
> And the rain-pools are the seas,
> And the leaves like little ships

135

Sail about on tiny trips;
And above the daisy tree
  Through the grasses,
High o'er head the Bumble Bee
  Hums and passes.

In that forest to and fro
I can wander, I can go;
See the spider and the fly,
And the ants go marching by
Carrying parcels with their feet
Down the green and grassy street.
I can in the sorrel sit
Where the ladybird alit.
I can climb the jointed grass;
  And on high
See the greater swallows pass
  In the sky,
And the round sun rolling by
Heeding no such things as I."

Another day he wrote,

"How do you like to go up in a swing,
  Up in the air so blue?
Oh, I do think it the pleasantest thing,
  Ever a child can do!

Up in the air and over the wall,
  Till I can see so wide,
Rivers and trees and cattle and all
  Over the countryside—

Till I look down on the garden green,
  Down on the roof so brown—
Up in the air I go flying again,
  Up in the air and down!"

Still another day he wrote,

"The gardener does not love to talk,
He makes me keep the gravel walk;
And when he puts his tools away,
He locks the door and takes the key.

Away behind the currant row,
Where no one else but cook may go,
Far in the plots, I see him dig,
Old and serious, brown and big.

He digs the flowers, green, red and blue,
Nor wishes to be spoken to.
He digs the flowers and cuts the hay,
And never seems to want to play."

These verses about his childhood Louis called "penny whistles." No one suspected that they would eventually be published as *A Child's Garden of Verses* and that children all over the world would read and love them years after he was dead. That summer he wrote fourteen of them.

Chapter XXIV

Bright is the ring of words
When the right man rings them,
Fair the fall of songs
When the singer sings them.

STILL THE RAIN rained, and the only diversions were books about Scotch history or games with Lloyd. Lloyd had now become an artist. The walls of the family sitting room were covered with his pictures.

The bad weather, however, bored him, too. All day he must remain in the house. In the evening his stepfather read dull articles aloud, or talked about Scottish history. Finally he was driven to complain.

"Louis," he said one night, "why don't you try to write something *interesting?*"

Everyone laughed.

"Well," said Louis. "Perhaps I should."

And indeed several days later he did just that. Again it was raining. He and Lloyd were painting. Idly Louis began to make a map of an island with many harbors. This island he called "Treasure Island." At various points he put interesting names, "Spy Glass Hill," "Skeleton Rock," etc.

Then in a moment of inspiration, he sat down and began to make a story around the island, the story of a boy who went to sea in search of buried treasure. That night, after tea, to a thrilled family he read the first chapter.

Other chapters followed thick and fast, one chapter a day. Everyone helped with it. His father wrote out for him a list of things that might be found in Billy Bones' chest. Lloyd and Fanny listened breathlessly to every word. The main character in the story, aside from the boy, was a sharp old sea cook with one leg, called "Long John Silver." This character had a faint resemblance to William Henley, the poet, the hearty, brilliant, one-legged Henley, who was Louis' great friend. And the book was called *The Sea Cook*.

A visitor came to Braemar, and insisted on taking the first nine chapters away with him to an editor in London. The editor wrote to say he would publish the story serially at once in *Young Folks* magazine, calling it *Treasure Island*. More chapters were to be sent in regularly.

But the excitement and the rain had their usual effect on Louis. He became ill, and had to leave Braemar suddenly, wearing a hateful rubber contraption on his nose, containing pine oil, to ease his breathing. Could anything be more humiliating than to travel by train through Scotland and England and France—all the way to Switzerland—in what Louis called a "pig's snout"?

So it was to be Davos again, the snowy mountain resort, this time in a chalet of their own, with their own cook, and great roaring fires to keep them warm.

Here Louis settled down to a winter of work and play. The work came first in a great gush—the remaining fourteen chapters of *Treasure Island* in fourteen days, more magazine articles, which he sent to Henley in London for a magazine he was editing. Nearly everything he wrote went to Colvin or Henley first. Gradually Henley became a sort of literary agent for him, suggesting publishers and magazines as Colvin had done. Having those two friends in London helped the wandering writer enormously.

Later Louis began to write a descriptive book about their stay at Juan Silverado, to be called *The Silverado Squatters*. Sometimes he wrote so much in one day that he must hold his pen between his second and third fingers to rest his hand. There were no typewriters in those days, and everything must be copied out by hand on big sheets of ruled paper.

Meanwhile, Lloyd came home from school for the

holidays and the two played games. This winter their game of warfare with the lead soldiers became elaborate. On the cold attic floor, lighted by a candle, they marched six hundred lead soldiers up and down a big stretch of country marked out on the floor in chalk, a country well-supplied with rivers, trees, hills, towns, and roads.

In the game four foot-soldiers or two cavalrymen equalled a regiment. Each man got as many shots as he had regiments in the field; but he could only fire when near enough to the enemy reasonably to do so. The shots were peas or cuff links, fired out of a popgun. After a single shot, one took one man off the field; a heavy shot brought down four men.

If one were not near enough to shoot, one must march and consolidate one's armies. Twelve inches of floor space equalled a day's march without artillery. Four inches meant a day's march with artillery. Bringing up food supplies was important and difficult.

The attic floor was very cold, and at last General Stevenson and General Osbourne must come downstairs again to the fire. Here they took up the art of printing, Lloyd doing the printing, Louis writing verses and illustrating them with pictures carved on blocks of wood. Making these woodcuts was great fun. Before they knew it, they had enough verses and woodcuts for a little book-let, called *Lay Morals,* which Lloyd printed and sold for sixpence.

By May the doctor said Louis was definitely better and need not return to Davos the next winter. But then he made the mistake of going back to Scotland. There, in the Highlands, and in the low country below Edinburgh, he undid all the good the winter in Switzerland had done him. The first few weeks he wrote one long story about a little French boy, called *The Treasure of Franchard,* but after that he grew rapidly worse. Early in September he had a serious hemorrhage from his lungs, and hurried back to France again, despairing of ever living in Scotland again.

This time he flatly refused to go to Davos. Instead they went to southern France overlooking the Mediterranean, to find as high a house as possible. For several months they lived in a house at St. Marcel near Marseilles, but in this house Louis was never well. By Christmas he fled to Nice in despair, and stayed there until the house at St. Marcel could be rented to someone else. Then they went to Hyères, farther along the coast, to a chalet above the town, called "Chalet La Solitude." Above them on the hillside was a ruined castle, in front of them the sea, all around the tiny chalet a "garden like a fairy-story," as Louis said.

"If you could only see my roses and my aloes, my fig-marigolds and my olives . . . my view of a certain mountain," he wrote to Gosse in London.

For nine months Louis lived a happy life in Hyères,

happy for the first time in many years. This period was always his real honeymoon to him, the time when life was sweet and friendly after years of hardship.

The first two weeks he wrote chiefly "penny whistles."

> "My bed is like a little boat;
>   Nurse helps me in when I embark;
> She girds me in my sailor's coat
>   And starts me in the dark.
>
> At night, I go on board and say
>   Good-night to all my friends on shore;
> I shut my eyes and sail away
>   And see and hear no more. . . ."

Another day he wrote,

> "The friendly cow all red and white,
>   I love with all my heart;
> She gives me cream with all her might,
>   To eat with apple-tart.
>
> She wanders lowing here and there,
>   And yet she cannot stray,
> All in the pleasant open air,
>   The pleasant light of day;

And blown by all the winds that pass
And wet with all the showers,
She walks among the meadow grass
And eats the meadow flowers."

By the middle of May he felt strong enough to begin
rewriting *Prince Otto,* the novel he had failed to finish
in Monterey. When this was done, he sold it for seven
hundred and fifty dollars.

How pleased he was to make this money. How he
gloated over being able to pay his own bills at last.

"I shall grow fat and rich yet," he said to Fanny.
"Become a regular 'guttler,' as Cummy would say."

Meanwhile, a further surprise was in store for him.
In May a publisher wrote to him offering five hundred
dollars for the book rights to *Treasure Island.* Louis said
yes, and the book was published at the end of November. To his amazement, people everywhere read this book
enthusiastically.

As a serial in *Young Folks* not many people read it.
In its book form it lay on the prime minister's table, in
the homes of judges, writers and soldiers. The editor of
the *Saturday Review,* a learned weekly, said it was the
best adventure story since *Robinson Crusoe.*

How happy it made Louis to be compared to that other
famous Scotchman! As an author, he was now making a
real success.

Chapter XXV

The ship rides trimmed, and from the eternal shore
Thou hearest airy voices; but not yet
Depart, my soul, not yet awhile depart.

FOR CHRISTMAS THAT year, Baxter and Henley came out to visit him. All Christmas week they celebrated his success in the chalet at Hyères. Then they went down to Nice to spend a few days in further celebration.

Within a few hours all the bright happiness was turned to gloom and anxiety. Louis caught cold in Nice, and the cold developed into pneumonia. Nothing more dangerous could have happened to him. Doctors came. Fanny came. Bob came. One by one they bent over him with anxious faces. Slowly, inch by inch, Louis fought back the disease.

By the first of January he was taken back to Hyères, and there he lay for many months, desperately ill. One night in May a dreadful hemorrhage came on late at night. Hearing him, Fanny rushed to his side with the medicine bottle and glass in her shaking hands. Seeing her tremble, Louis took a piece of paper and a pencil from the table, and wrote,

"Don't be frightened; if this is death, it is an easy one."

Then he took the bottle and glass from her, measured out the medicine quietly, and handed the bottle back with a gentle smile.

But the effects of that night lingered. Louis' right arm was strapped down to his side, so that his right lung would not move; he was forbidden to speak at all. The room in which he lay was in darkness.

In this pitiable state, he wrote more "penny whistles" in the old brown notebook. One day, thinking of the times he had been ill and frightened as a child, he wrote,

"The world is so great, and I am so small,
I do not like it at all, at all."

After writing those words, he stopped and looked at them for a moment. Then he lifted his pencil and crossed them out, writing beneath them,

"The world is so full of a number of things
I am sure we should all be as happy as kings."

With this beginning, he finished the poem in the form it is now known to everyone.

How gay, how whimsical Louis was in those days of

great illness. Everyone who saw him commented on it. The battle, however, lasted too long for him to keep quite the same gallant, whimsical spirit. For three years thereafter Louis remained in tragic health, becoming so thin as to look almost spectral, dressing in the careless, slovenly fashion of an invalid—and writing some remarkably good books.

Most of those three years he spent in England, for in June he came over slowly from Hyères to settle in the seaside town of Bournemouth on the south coast. Lloyd was in school at Bournemouth, and it was near enough to London for Louis' friends to come down to see him. Also his father could be with him there some of the time, an important factor, since Mr. Thomas Stevenson was now in failing health. His mind was beginning to be clouded; an unnatural sadness made him silent and helpless.

At first the Stevensons lived in lodgings, with Louis lying in bed, fretting. It was only when Henley came down, with his crutch and his red beard, to write plays with him, that he cheered up noticeably. In November they moved into a furnished house. There Louis was able to do some work, first a magazine story of the gruesome variety, called *Olalla,* then the final drafts of *A Child's Garden of Verses,* the rest of *Prince Otto* and *More New Arabian Nights,* which he began at Hyères in collaboration with his wife. The fact that he was able to work at all encouraged him a great deal.

143

Thinking that Bournemouth was probably a good place for his son, Mr. Stevenson bought a house there for him in January. The house was to be called Skerryvore after one of the more famous lighthouses Mr. Stevenson had built. While he was waiting for it to be put in order, Louis gathered together all of those fragments of Highland history he had been accumulating for so long, and began to write a Highland story.

Meanwhile in March *A Child's Garden of Verses* was published, a modest green book which none of Louis' friends took very seriously. No one dreamed what success it would have. Until the children of the world discovered how lovely the poems were, the grown-up world passed them over lightly. Yet now today, more than fifty years later, they are read with delight by old and young.

While the poems were waiting for recognition, the Stevenson family moved into their new home. The house itself was a suburban villa outside the town. It had belonged to an old sea captain. Outside, it had a small stable, a tiny carriage house, a large dovecote on the lawn, and a pleasant garden where Woggs might romp. Inside, it was roomy and comfortable.

"Our drawing-room," wrote Louis to a friend, "is now a place so beautiful it is like eating to sit in it. No other room is so lovely in the world; there I sit like an old Irish beggarman . . . in a palace throne-room."

And indeed everyone who saw Louis at that time agreed that he was a pathetic figure. Once he moved into the house, he scarcely left it for three years, not even to go to his own garden gate or down into the town of Bournemouth. Everyone must come to him—the barber who cut his hair, friends from London, neighbors who loved to hear his brilliant talk.

Much of the time he lay in bed, where he did most of his writing. Downstairs he was a pale, emaciated man in any old clothes, a shawl around his shoulders, his hair long, his eyes sombre. When he was too ill to work he played, sometimes, on a penny whistle; when that was forbidden, he began to model little figures in clay, saying that he should have been a sculptor, since it was fascinating work.

Still the illness persisted. Secretly his family and friends wondered if he ever would be well again. They longed to get a good photograph of him. Amateur photography was a new art at that time. Lloyd had a camera. Their friend, Sir Percy Shelley (son of the poet) also had a camera. Whenever it was possible, Louis sat out on the terrace for a few minutes to have his picture taken, but the results always showed too plainly the sick man.

"Do you remember," he wrote afterward to a friend, "the pallid brute that lived in Skerryvore like a weevil in a biscuit?"

Chapter XXVI

So awhile I glowed, and then
Fell on dusty days and men;
Long I slumbered packed in straw,
Long I none but dealers saw.

ONCE OR TWICE that summer—he was now thirty-four—
Louis tried to take a short trip away from home. Each
time the trip ended abruptly in a hemorrhage that
brought him hurrying back to bed.

Meanwhile he was not writing as much as he wished.
Sometimes he must ask his father for money. This made
him anxious: at night he lay troubled about how he
could do more writing. In this state of anxiety stories
sometimes came to him.

One night he had such a waking-dream about a man
who led a double life. By day this man was a respectable
doctor; at night, by taking some strong medicine, he became an ugly, dwarfish creature, capable of any cruelty.
In this state one night, he killed a man. Everyone who

has read Stevenson's books knows the story of *Dr. Jekyll and Mr. Hyde.*

Awakening from his dream, Louis reached for paper in the early dawn, and for three days hardly stopped writing. Chapter after chapter of the great story flowed from his fingers. He came down to lunch like a man in a dream, and in the late afternoon, when he could write no more, lay on his bed in a kind of stupor, waiting for more energy.

Fanny watched him anxiously during those days. She wondered if he could stand the strain. Physically alone, it was a great strain to write ten thousand words a day as he was doing. But a greater strain than the writing lay ahead. Fanny did not approve of the story when it was written. Her face lengthened as she read it. Writing out her criticism on paper, as she always did, she gave it to him and left the room.

Perhaps the criticism was too harsh; perhaps Louis was over-sensitive. At any rate, when she came back later, Louis was sitting up in bed, fresh paper on his knee, a thermometer sticking out of his mouth, and a pile of ashes on the hearth to which he pointed accusingly.

Fanny cried out that she did not mean for him to destroy his manuscript. He answered grimly that he *must* destroy it after what she had said. And so he went to work again, and rewrote the whole story in three days, after that revising more slowly.

Dr. Jekyll and Mr. Hyde was first printed as a paper-backed novel to sell for a shilling (twenty-five cents). By January it lay on the bookstalls, awaiting notice. At first it sold slowly. Then *The London Times,* a venerable newspaper, printed a review of it, saying it was a splendid story. People began to read it. Like *Treasure Island* two years before, it caught hold suddenly. Everyone was gripped by the power of its narrative. In six months forty thousand copies had been sold in England alone. The pale, spectral author, with his medicine bottle on the shelf and the blood on his handkerchief, had made a second great success.

Meanwhile, down in Bournemouth, Louis was very busy, not celebrating his success, but writing the boy's book he had started and laid aside the spring before.

This new book came to him easily. His hand seemed to write the story for him, the story of a boy in the Highland country in the troubled days of 1751, fleeing from the soldiers lest he be arrested for a murder he did not commit. Every inch of the wild Highland country seemed to be in the story. Even Earraid, the little island where Louis groaned as an engineering student, became a part of this fine tale. *Kidnapped,* the adventures of David Balfour, was the new book Stevenson wrote.

Kidnapped was published serially in the magazine, *Young Folks,* from May to July, then brought out in book form. Its success was instantaneous. Readers were enchanted with this clever Scottish writer, this Robert Louis Stevenson who produced one thrilling tale after another.

"There," they said, "is a strong, active man who must lead a hearty life."

They could see him striding the hills in the Highlands with a gun on his shoulder, buffeted by the weather.

The man in his bed at Bournemouth smiled when he heard these comments.

For the rest of that year, Louis did not do much writing. His spirit flagged. His health was not good. Also the care of his father was becoming more and more a problem for them all. Mr. Stevenson was now completely broken in health, with a mind that was very much clouded.

As he grew worse during the winter it seemed best to take him back to Edinburgh. Early in the new year he went back to his old home in Heriot Row. And there he died on the ninth of May, two days after Louis arrived in a shaky state to be with him.

Louis tried to help, but almost immediately was forced to go to bed. It was several weeks before Fanny was able to get him back to Bournemouth. Once he got there, however, he decided one thing quite suddenly. Bournemouth did *not* agree with him. Apparently no place in

England had sun and dry air enough to heal his diseased lungs. Some place far away must be found, if he was to "die in a ditch" as he had boasted, instead of in his bed in the nightshirt he had come to hate.

In addition to his feeling that Bournemouth did not have a climate that suited him, the thought of a trip somewhere, anywhere, brought a sweet taste to his mouth. Robert Louis Stevenson, the treasure hunter, the man of adventure always!

And so it was decided to start again for America, to the high mountains in the west, to the flat dry deserts, somewhere where he could find new health and vigor. The family party this time would be large: Louis, his wife, Lloyd, his mother, a faithful French maid, Valentine. All five of them gathered in London on August twenty-first, prepared to sail in the morning for a new land. The year was 1887; Louis was now thirty-six years old.

The Singing Heart

Chapter XXVII

When snipes are silent in the frozen bogs,
And all the garden garth is whelmed in mire
Lo, by the hearth, the laughter of the logs—
More fair than roses, lo, the flowers of fire.

THE TRIP TO America was exciting and wonderful. No sooner were they started than Louis felt better. How thrilling that was after years of illness. Perhaps, after all, he could some day be a well man.

Meanwhile, the voyage itself was very interesting. The boat on which they traveled was a cargo boat, loaded with horses and cows and monkeys and matches. What fun they all had watching the monkeys and horses. How amusing it was to see one old baboon choose Louis for his friend, and follow him solemnly around the deck.

Then there were the sailors to watch, the tarry smell of the ship, the sea all around them. Boldly Louis announced on the second day that boating was his favorite sport, that he meant to spend the rest of his life at sea!

159

"I had forgotten," he wrote to Bob, "what happiness was. My heart literally sings."

With his heart still singing, although he did have a slight cold by then, he arrived in New York early in September.

There a great surprise awaited him. When the ship drew into anchor, a large crowd of newspaper reporters came on board to meet him. The American people, they said, had read his books. They knew he was a great writer. They wanted to know how he looked, what he wore, what he ate for breakfast, how long he would be in New York.

Moreover, another surprise was in store for him. Fame in America, he discovered, would bring him a golden harvest of money. His American publisher, Mr. Scribner, was ready to bring out a new and handsome edition of *Treasure Island*. He wanted him to write a dozen articles for his magazine during the winter, at three hundred dollars apiece. He was ready to pay eight thousand dollars for the magazine serial rights to his next book. This was what success in America meant.

How different this all was from the last time Louis arrived in New York. How different it all was from the eight difficult, dangerous years in between, years in bed, years of hard work, years of wandering in search of health. A little conscious of his rumpled jacket and

trousers, Louis wondered if it was still the same man inside of them, or merely a dream-man.

Fanny, however, knew that he was the same man—her
lovable, carelessly dressed, brilliant sick man. She felt
that she must get him quickly away to a high, dry climate where his lungs would continue to heal. Louis himself was perfectly willing to go. His feeling about
"Noah's Ark" dinner parties had not changed. He would
always be the same wandering, restless artist.

Considering where the best climate for him might be,
his American friends suggested Saranac Lake in the
Adirondack Mountains of New York, instead of mountains farther west. And so there they went, Fanny and
Lloyd first, to rent half of a small house on a hill overlooking the Saranac River, his mother and Louis afterward on a special train provided by the railroad.

Saranac itself in those days was a simple, backwoods
village of wooden houses. Not a piece of gray slate in
the whole village! That fact in itself made Scotland seem
very far away. But Louis was used by now to being far
away from Scotland. His "ain gray town" had become
a dream-town, existing only in his memory. Twenty years
since he had been a student there in the University.
Many more since he had outgrown Cummy and his childhood home.

Louis called the house where they lived in Saranac his

"hatbox on the hill." The rooms which they occupied were mainly on the ground floor. There was the living room with an open fireplace, where they also took their meals. There was his mother's bedroom, his and Fanny's bedroom, and a tiny room where he might work.

How cold it already was in Saranac in October. No sooner had they arrived than Fanny set out for Canada to buy furs for them all for the winter. In a very short time the snow came, and Louis was striding up and down the veranda in a buffalo coat, a fur cap and Indian moccasins.

"I walk on my verandy in the snaw," he wrote to Colvin.

Inside, in his workroom, he worked at his battered desk until his fingers were stiff with cold, in spite of the roaring stove; then he played on the piano or a penny whistle to warm them. The maid and his wife and mother struggled to keep house in country fashion.

Louis himself was happy and cheerful. When the doctor recommended large glasses of egg-nog for him, he looked a little doubtfully at the bowl of eggs, but decided he could drink them. Tidy, the cow, had provided the milk. Tying on an apron, he beat the raw eggs up with a fork, waving it in the air between beatings.

As he wrote to Colvin at Christmas-time, he was "sa cockered up and healthy" in the new climate, he felt he could do anything. Where were the hemorrhages of

162

Bournemouth days, of Switzerland, of southern France? He could hardly believe that the blood had ceased to come up in his mouth.

Meanwhile his work was going well. The monthly magazine articles came to him easily. Already he had started on a new adventure story. Remembering an old story of his uncle's about an Indian magician buried alive and dug up again, still breathing, he began to write the story of two Scottish brothers in which the incident might be used. How easily he drew on his knowledge of Scottish life and character for this grim book, which was to be called *The Master of Ballantrae.*

Lloyd also was writing a book, *The Wrong Box,* as they eventually called it. Louis helped him with this, too.

After the first of January, however, the cold became more bitter, and this troubled them all. The thermometer often reached ten degrees below zero. The snow lay up to the window ledges, and the windows themselves were caulked with cotton. Inside the family huddled around the fireplace in the living room, with their feet on logs of wood to keep them off the drafty floor. A fur coat on the back of the kitchen door froze to it during the night. Louis' bottle of ink also froze at night. Fanny was so unwell in the mountain climate she went away on several trips, and planned a trip to California in March. As always, Louis began to weary of the one place, the one way of doing.

This feeling of restlessness made him think he would like to make a cruise when summer came. Yachts and yachting were expensive, but he had already made so much money in America, it could be done. Should they cruise in the Atlantic or the Pacific Ocean? Loving maps as he did, it was fun to pore over the *Directories of the World* at night, planning a cruise.

The plans became more definite in March, however, when a new American publisher, Mr. McClure, came to see him, and asked him to make a unique trip as soon as he was able. He wanted Louis to cruise for several months among the South Sea Islands of the Pacific, in order to write a series of travel letters about them for his news-paper, the New York *Sun*. The man who had walked for ten days in France with a donkey, and had written a charming travel book about his adventures there, was to cruise for six months among savage and cannibal islands and describe his adventures. What a book that should make!

Would the doctor let him go? By the middle of April he would be ready to say yes or no. The great day came, and the doctor said yes, the lungs were healed enough for him to leave Saranac. In a great burst of joy and relief at this news, Louis wrote thirty-five letters in one day to his friends in all parts of the world.

164

Chapter XXVIII

I should like to rise and go
Where the golden apples grow;—
Where below another sky
Parrot islands anchored lie.

WHERE WERE THE South Sea Islands? How many of them were there? Louis and Lloyd got out a book to see, for Fanny had already started for California.

"Gravy, Lloyd," said Louis, using Cummy's old expression, "there are hundreds of them, all as big as pin-points on the map. Do savage tribes live on all of these pin-points?"

"They must," said Lloyd, bending over the map. "The book says they do. And I can see from the map that they're going to be warm and jolly. South of the equator they are, in the middle of the Pacific Ocean. We'll have to go south from San Francisco to get to them. It must be hot there all the year around."

"Brrr!" said Louis, shivering a little. "That won't be

hard to bear after a winter in the Adirondacks, will it? I would like to stay in a warm country a long time after this winter."

"Me, too," said Lloyd. "And anyhow we'll be going from island to island. We ought to see a lot."

"Cannibals, perhaps," said Louis, reading out of the book. "And lepers just as there were in the Bible. And pearl divers, and cocoanut trees, and funny fishes."

"I'm sure we'll get some queer things to eat," said Lloyd.

"Well, after this winter," said Louis a little ruefully, "and all our other trips together, we should be able to eat some odd food without minding it. When I think of all the queer food I have eaten in my life, I could write a book about that alone."

"You haven't begun to eat the queer food you're going to eat," said Louis' mother, smiling. "You're just a little boy at home, eating rabbit pie, compared to what you're going to be."

"That is true, mother," said Louis, "but as long as you're going with us, what does it matter?"

The cruise to the South Sea Islands did not begin until the last of June. First they must rent a yacht. While Louis visited friends in New Jersey, Fanny looked for a yacht in San Francisco. One fine day she telegraphed that she had found one, a glistening white ship with room for all

166

the family, the captain and his wife, four sailors and a cook.

The cost of the cruise was going to be enormous. Seven hundred and fifty dollars a month to rent the yacht, wages for six people, food for a dozen. In six or seven months Louis would spend ten thousand dollars. Would the money he received for his travel letters cover all this expense? Apparently it would.

In San Francisco they bought clothes for the trip, strange, summery clothes for a hot climate. Louis, in white trousers and a white shirt and a red scarf around his waist, would look very handsome. The ladies bought full, muslin dresses called "mumus." Then, too, they must buy food for the journey: tin boxes of crackers, cans of beef, barrels of salt pork, syrup, potatoes, flour.

The yacht itself belonged to a wealthy man. It was very beautiful, with white sails, white decks, brass fittings, red silk in the cabin, lace curtains in front of the berths, many mirrors. No one doubted that it could go anywhere and do anything.

And so they set sail from San Francisco three thousand miles across the Pacific Ocean for a group of islands called the Marquesas.

The voyage lasted four weeks. How exciting it all was. The yacht had an open cockpit in the stern, which was their outdoor sitting room. Here they sat during the day, and played cards after dinner in the evening. Inside, in

167

the red-silk cabin they ate their meals and slept in the berths behind the lace curtains. But what they were all waiting for was the first sight of the Marquesas, the first tropical island of the South Seas.

The big moment, when it came, came suddenly. Before the sun was up one morning they all gathered in the open cockpit to watch for land. Gradually the sky lightened in front of them. Pink and gold rays of the sun crept up over the horizon. And then there was the island of Nukahiva, lovely rose- and olive- and pearl-colored cliffs, crowned with green forest.

Sailing slowly around the edge of this island, they came to a little cove in a sandy beach down below the mountains and the green forest. Edging the beach grew green palm trees, "the giraffe among vegetables," as Louis called them. Underneath these green trees was a village of native houses which could hardly be seen from the ship. But what they did see on the shore, running tamely around like pet dogs, were a number of small, active pigs. Also in the trees of the forest strange birds sang. As they came closer Louis' mother said she saw a flash of scarlet and white feathers on a flying bird.

As soon as they were well within the cove, the captain dropped anchor and they all waited to see what would happen next. They did not have long to wait. In a few minutes a canoe put out from shore, and soon the water all around them was swarming with canoes. In these canoes sat brown-skinned, tattooed men, holding up home-made things to sell—mats and baskets and crude weapons. Some of them spoke a few words of English, for one white trader lived on their island in order to buy dried cocoanut meat, called copra, from them. Making copra was the chief industry of the islands.

When they found the Stevenson family would not buy their trinkets, the islanders were angry at first. Louis, however, invited them to come on board to drink syrup-and-water and eat crackers spread with jam. That made friends of them all. The islanders loved the sweet, sticky food of the white men.

For three weeks Louis and his family lived on the yacht in the cove, going ashore each day to explore the island. The chickens on this tropical island, they discovered, were wild and lived in the woods. One must hunt a long time for their eggs. The pigs, on the other hand, lived with the family like pet dogs, and stole morsels of food when they could. They even swam in the ocean after their owners! Fish were caught with bare hands in shallow water.

After trying vainly to catch fish in this way, Louis contented himself with gathering shells on the beach "in the silver margin of the sea," as he said. The shells themselves were all colors of the rainbow; sometimes they

169

were as large as a woman's head. In a thick notebook Louis wrote down all that he saw on his trips ashore.

Fanny, meanwhile, was very busy keeping house for her family. All of them now drank cocoanut milk freely and ate the cooked cocoanut meat from the shells. Fish they had in great plenty. There was also a native vegetable called breadfruit, which was something like a potato in flavor and looked like a large melon. When it was roasted in the fire and broken open, the white core came out tender and mealy, and could be eaten with a sauce of creamed cocoanut. Served in this way, it tasted something like creamed potatoes.

After leaving Nukahiva, the yacht sailed to other islands of the Marquesas, stopping once for twelve days and again for shorter periods. What strange things they saw and learned. When the native chiefs were pleased with Louis they gave him a lock of hair from an old man's beard to wear in his hat. Cannibalism, he learned, the custom of eating enemies slain in battle, had been forbidden recently by the French, who owned the islands. But once Louis did go up the mountain through the forest to a special place where such feasts of "long pig," as a man was called, had been held.

All this, and pleasanter facts, he wrote down faithfully in his notebook. The days passed quickly. Meanwhile they were all getting very brown, faces, hands and feet, for they went barefoot a good deal. But it was time now to sail three days' journey to another group of islands, the Paumotus, west and south of the Marquesas.

The journey there proved difficult. The yacht, tall and slender, could not stand up against the strong tropical winds. She was often blown off her course. Rocks and reefs under the water made the passage dangerous.

The Paumotus are low, flat islands made of coral and covered with palm trees. No wooded mountains and colored cliffs here at all. There was plenty of strong sunshine, however, which made everything about the islands pink and shimmering.

The natives of Fakarava, the island where they stayed the longest, called the yacht "the silver ship" because it shone so brightly in the sunlight. To the Stevensons, however, she was fast becoming a source of trouble and anxiety, because she was so hard to sail in tropical seas.

Coming into the one harbor of Fakarava, which was shaped like the mouth of a fish, everyone rushed to the side of the ship to see the wonderful things down under the water. Masses of pink coral branching like trees far below them. Schools of rainbow-colored fish with strange patterns on them. One of these fish had a beak like a parrot.

Here on the island of Fakarava the Stevensons spent two weeks, sleeping in a bungalow on the shore at night because the nights on board the yacht were warm; riding horseback or gathering shells on the beach by day. Louis himself spent a good deal of time with a half-caste Frenchman, who was vice-president of the island under the French government. From him he learned a great deal about the native customs, how these strange, simple brown men lived and acted.

Chapter XXIX

I came, not hoping, and, like one
Snatched out of blindness. rubbed my eyes,
And hailed my promised land with cries.

WEST OF THE Paumotu Islands in the great Pacific Ocean
lie the Society Islands. It was here the Stevensons went
next on their cruise. The Society Islands, like the Marquesas, are mountainous islands with a rim of blue sea
and sandy shore around their edges. Like the Marquesas,
too, they are very beautiful, very warm and mild, very
full of color and strange native life.

The largest island of them all, Tahiti, is the most
famous. It was here the yacht steered its course from
Fakarava to the seaport town of Papeete. But Louis had
caught cold in Fakarava, and on reaching Papeete became increasingly ill. A week on shore in the warm, sticky
air did him no good at all. So he boarded the yacht again,
the silver ship which gave so much trouble in these
tropical waters, and sailed around the island to the village
of Taravao.

Taravao proved worse than Papeete. It was hot and full of mosquitoes. In a short time Louis was burning up with malaria, and coughing badly. Also they discovered that the jib-boom on the yacht had sprung, and needed repairs. What were they to do?

Fanny, as usual, acted with great energy. Going ashore, she found her way to a Chinaman's shanty, and rented from him a wagon and a team of horses. Bringing Louis ashore and putting him in the wagon, they drove sixteen miles along the coast to the village of Tautira. Twenty-one times on this journey they came to a mountain stream flowing across the road, but each time they managed to wade through it. In the end they got Louis to Tautira into a house that seemed comfortable.

The next day, however, a native princess, Princess Moë, came to see the sick white man, and insisted that he be carried to the house of the village chief, Ori. Ori's house, like all the others, was built up on a platform. It was round and made of bamboo poles. It looked, Louis said, like a giant birdcage. In this giant birdcage, he was laid tenderly in a native bed.

It was not long before his health mended. The tropical climate, apparently, agreed with him perfectly. In a few days he was out on the beach, barefooted, in a suit of flannel pajamas, and after a few more days he actually went bathing in the warm surf. Soon he was able to work again, gathering native ballads for his book, writing ballads of his own. He and Ori, a handsome man, brown as a piece of polished wood, became great friends. From Ori, Louis learned a great deal about the island.

Before they left Tahiti, Louis also began working again on *The Master of Ballentrae* which he had begun at Saranac. One reason why he was eager to finish this book was that he was beginning to worry a good deal about money. The yacht had arrived at Tautira with her jib-boom mended, only to have it discovered that her two masts were rotten. With one blow of his fist the captain broke one of these unsound masts completely in two. It was, therefore, necessary for the yacht to crawl away for repairs, while the Stevenson family stayed on in Tautira indefinitely.

Another source of worry was the South Sea book. Louis wanted to put his material into a huge travel book. Fanny said that he should write romantic tales about the South Seas, not a descriptive volume. Whichever it should be, however, it was plain that the writing would take much longer than he had planned. And meanwhile he was spending money like water on a crippled yacht. No wonder he wrote furiously on his story of the two Scotch brothers in *The Master of Ballantrae*.

Weeks went by, and still the yacht did not return. Their money and provisions gave out. Ori must now supply them with native food. For lunch one day there was raw fish with cocoanut milk poured over it and roasted bananas. For weeks they had been drinking cocoanut cream in their coffee. Louis said that if anyone were to set a dish of boiled turnips in front of him he would cry! These troubles, however, did not prevent him from enjoying the wonderful, warm climate and the sea bathing. Nor did they really go hungry, for there were young pigs, eggs, cocoanuts, bananas, wild chickens and breadfruit to eat.

December came, and at last the yacht got back to Tautira. On Christmas day they were able to sail away for the Sandwich Islands up on the other side of the equator. The trip took thirty days, because the passage was stormy. Fanny began to doubt if she liked the sea as well as Louis did.

The Sandwich Islands were not as wild and primitive as the other islands had been. In fact, the main city on the main island—Honolulu on the island of Hawaii—was in some ways like a dirty American town. Nevertheless it was a picturesque, fascinating town, a typical tropical city, with white men and brown men living in it side by side. And all the world knows how gloriously the sun sets in Hawaii.

Paying off the yacht with something of a feeling of relief, Louis and his family moved into a native house on the beach at Waikiki, four miles along the coast from Honolulu. This native house had four small rooms and a lanai. A lanai is an open-air living room, open on three sides, excepting for a screen of flowering vines. How luxuriously the flowers grew in Hawaii. Every tree and house and garden hung with brilliant flowers. In the groves of palm trees, too, peacocks screamed and spread their plumage.

The climate, however, was colder than in the islands farther south. In their open-air living room, the family shivered a little, forgetting entirely how much colder they had been in Saranac, in Switzerland, and in Scotland.

In a shack behind the lanai Louis worked each day. He also entertained a little mouse there, for soon one came to sit on a shelf and watch him. A friend passing the shack one evening saw Louis lying on his bed, gravely playing his flute to the little mouse. Lizards, too, crawled up and down the walls of the shack, which were papered with newspaper.

Meanwhile, how hard he worked to finish *The Master of Ballantrae*. It was a fine, stern book, one of the best he had done, save for the last few chapters. How eagerly readers on both sides of the Atlantic would welcome it. A new book by Robert Louis Stevenson was a literary event of great importance. The author in his shack in Hawaii never quite realized this. He merely wrote faith-fully each day, and wondered whether he should go home in June or off on another cruise among the islands. The health which he had found in the South Seas was the most precious possession he had.

What he did next depended a good deal on how his bank account stood at home. Charles Baxter received and banked all the money that came to him from his books. In March a letter came, saying that he still had money in the bank. The costly cruise on the yacht had not swallowed up all his savings.

Relieved of this anxiety, he began to enjoy Hawaii more. There was much to enjoy in Hawaii. The music, for example. Everywhere one went there was music and dancing. With his quick enthusiasm Lloyd had begun to play the Hawaiian musical instruments. He had a violin, a banjo, and a Hawaiian guitar now, as well as numbers of song books.

There was a native king in Hawaii, too—King David Kalakaua, who lived in a native palace. King David was a fat, brown man with drooping moustaches, who wore an embroidered coat. Louis became his great friend, and often visited him in his palace, or played cards with him in a summer-house in the palace grounds.

One day an Englishman in the settlement gave a feast in honor of Robert Louis Stevenson. King David and his sister came. All the guests sat on mats on the floor, and ate their food very politely. The food itself was strange: chicken and cocoanut tied up together in leaves and roasted; pork and beef and salmon cooked together; another kind of fish cooked with clams; next a kind of edible seaweed, boiled; finally sweet-potato pudding.

"Everything that grows on land or sea," said Louis afterward. "If they forgot anything, I don't know what it could be."

At the feast, however, he tried to eat some of everything, and afterward gave King David a golden pearl for a present.

"To golden hands the golden pearl I bring, the ocean jewel to the island king," he said in presenting it.

How well Louis was able to fit into a South Sea island scene. Although he was now a famous author, he was still the same gay, foolish Louis who had carved a face on the cheese at Walter Simpson's long ago. "Noah's Ark" parties would still have been boring to him, if he had gone to them.

Chapter XXX

I heard the pulse of the besieging sea
Throb far away all night. I heard the wind
Fly crying and convulse tumultuous palms.

THE TIME TO leave Hawaii was drawing near. Already Louis had decided to go on another cruise among savage islands, instead of going home to England. *The Master of Ballantrae* was finished and off to the publishers. Before he left Hawaii, however, he wanted to visit the leper colony on the island of Molokai, another of the Sandwich Islands not far away.

All through the South Seas they had seen lepers. Sick men wandering on the beach with strange, silvery faces, and sores tied up in rags. Men hopeless of being cured, as men had been in Biblical times two thousand years ago. Louis knew what it meant to be dangerously ill. His heart ached for these sick men and women and children, for there were some of all three.

In Hawaii and some of the more civilized islands, lepers were not left to roam the beach, but were taken to

Molokai for treatment and isolation. Here Louis went for a two weeks' visit in May. The leper settlement in Molokai was surrounded by a bamboo fence, but within its boundaries the people had a good deal of freedom. Louis did not land directly at the dock nearest the colony when he arrived. Instead he passed on to another part of the island, and then rode back leisurely for two days on horseback through the mountains.

Arriving, he met the doctors and priests and nuns in charge of the patients. They gave him a shack of his own to sleep in, in an isolated place. In the daytime he rode over on horseback to see the sick people, not all of whom were in bed. Afterward he played croquet with six little leper girls, or watched them sew for their dolls. In a letter to Colvin he begged him to send out scraps of silk for this dolls' dressmaking.

Everyone at Molokai was eager to tell him about one leper who had died there a few weeks before. This was Father Damien, a Belgian priest who came out to the island a strong, healthy man sixteen years before to pray and preach for the people.

When he got there, however, Father Damien found that there was much beside preaching needed. The lepers were poorly housed, their food was not good, their supply of water uncertain. With his own strong peasant hands Father Damien set about improving these conditions. Working alongside the sick men, who had built most of

181

their own village, he helped to make things more comfortable. Following his example, other priests came out to help him.

Under the circumstances it was not surprising that Father Damien himself contracted leprosy. Doctors had warned him that he might. But, as long as his health lasted, he continued to work at the leper colony, a bluff, hearty man much loved by the other patients. When Louis Stevenson came out, they were still mourning his death there.

Meanwhile, back in Hawaii, Fanny had been getting ready for their next cruise. This time they were to sail on a trading schooner, not a yacht of their own. The schooner was to take them to the Gilbert Islands south of Hawaii, and on perhaps to China.

Storms and squalls kept them from carrying out all of this plan. But they did visit the Gilbert Islands, after a wild, rough trip, and from there went on to the Samoan Islands. During the rough passages by sea, the ship rolled and tossed. On shore they found it hot and muggy. Nevertheless, they had a good time in spite of their difficulties. Louis no longer thought of wearing white shirts or yachting trousers now. All of them, even Fanny, went barefoot most of the time. Like the natives, they wore strings of flowers, of seeds or shells around their necks. A gypsy family indeed.

The Gilbert Islands were not at that time owned by

any outside nation. A native king ruled over each separate island. This made it much more dangerous to live
on shore among the natives, but Louis and his family did
so for weeks at a time. After landing on the first island,
and allowing the schooner to sail away, they discovered
that the natives had been having a festival and were
drunk and bad-tempered. What should Louis do? In
great anxiety he visited the native king and begged him
to forbid further drinking. Only after ten days did he
agree to do this.

Leaving this island when the schooner came back for
them, they went on to the island of Apemama. Here a
native king, King Tembinok', ruled over his people.
King Tembinok' was a fierce, dark-skinned man with a
hawk-like face. He often carried a rifle in his hands and
shot at anyone who displeased him. Before going ashore
this time, Louis sent a messenger to the king to ask if he
would be their friend and help them. After two days of
doubt he sent back word that he would.

Moving ashore under his protection, they arranged to
live in four bamboo cabins and a dining shed behind the
palace in a grove of palm trees. Natives buzzed around
this new home all day, but did not come too close, for
the king had forbidden it. The island itself, like the
Paumotus, was low and flat, a pink and white island,
feathered with palm trees.

Every morning King Tembinok' sent them presents of

food for the day. Twelve shells of cocoanut sap to drink; twelve empty kerosene cans of fresh water; salt pork and beef; turtle meat; bad rice; boiled roots that tasted like sweet potatoes. Under a great tent of mosquito netting the whole family sat at mealtime and ate this queer food.

Once the king gave them a banquet at which he served his finest dishes. The menu was as follows: turtle soup, turtle steak, fish, wild chicken tasting like fish, a young roasted pig, cocoanut salad, roasted cocoanut shoots for dessert. With this food there was served expensive French wine. How on earth did a savage king get wine from France?

Tembinok', Louis learned, was a great trader. Every trading-ship in the South Seas knew that he was wealthy and would buy anything they brought him. His palace was stuffed with possessions. Behind the palace, which consisted of twenty houses, he had a great shed full of things he could not use—clocks, bowls, sewing-machines, a rocking-horse, ladies' parasols. Bolts of cloth and fancy uniforms were his delight.

His own clothes were never twice the same. Embroidered green velvet trousers, red-silk jackets, much gold braid, fancy helmets on his coarse black hair, nothing was too bright and gaudy for him. For two months the Stevenson family lived as his guests, and learned much about life in the Gilbert Islands.

The schooner came back for them, and they left Apemama. The bad weather now made it impossible for them to go on to China. Instead they went south to the more civilized Samoan Islands, where they left the schooner and stayed two months in Apia on the island of Upolu. There were three hundred white men in Apia, quite a white colony.

How strange the Stevenson family looked as they landed in Apia. People asked each other who this white family was, brown and burnt by the sun, barefooted, hung with musical instruments. First the tall, thin man in short sleeves and dirty trousers, carrying a camera. Then the woman with sea-shells round her hat, wearing a bright shawl and carrying a mandolin. Then the young man in striped pajamas and sun-glasses, carrying a banjo and a guitar.

Robert Louis Stevenson, the famous author, and his family, just returned from a five months' cruise! Wasn't there some story of his having been tubercular, confined to his bed for years? Not much like that now.

In a short time they were settled in a wooden cottage in the town, with Louis making more and more notes for his thick book on the South Seas. He also wrote one short story, *The Bottle Imp*, later published in a book of South Sea stories called *Island Nights Entertainments*. Lloyd, too, was writing a book, *The Wrecker*; Louis was helping him with that.

185

And in Apia a great idea came to Louis. He would buy a piece of land on this island, build a cottage on it, and come here every winter from England to protect his precious health. Samoa was on the direct route to Australia; ships going back and forth stopped at Apia frequently. With this idea in mind, he bought three hundred acres of wooded land on the mountainside behind Apia, three miles up a rough path from the town. But he was anxious to get home now, on to Australia for his mail, and from there home to England where his friends were. It was two and a half years since he had seen any of them.

Making arrangements for some of his new land to be cleared while he was gone, he sailed eagerly away from the tropics to Australia. There would be fires in Australia and some rain and cold wind in February. How odd that would seem.

But there was more than rain and cold wind waiting for him in Australia. There was waiting also the cold, unwelcome discovery that he could not stand a temperate climate any more than he ever could. As soon as he reached Australia, he caught cold, and in a few days he had a hemorrhage from his lungs. Again Fanny was a busy, frantic nurse with a sick man on her hands.

The most pressing question was what to do next. In his condition, Louis did not dare start for England. Nor did he dare stay in Australia, although he was too ill to make much effort to go anywhere else. The only possible solution lay in getting aboard the first ship they could, and going back to the islands, any islands in the warm South Seas. This is what they did, on a steam trading vessel that did not want to carry passengers at all, but took the Stevenson family in order to save Louis' life.

Chapter XXXI

Long must elapse ere you behold again
Green forest frame the entry of the lane
The wild lane with the bramble and the briar
The year-old cart-tracks perfect in the mire.

THE FOLLOWING MONTHS of cruising were different from the others. Louis was now traveling as an exile, a man cut off from home. Slowly, surely, this truth sank into his mind. He had come out to the other side of the world on a trip, and now he would never go back. On the side of a mountain in far-away Samoa he must make a new home.

After the first shock of realizing this, he was not visibly unhappy. After all, he liked the islands and island life. But on the cruise of the *Janet Nicoll* he could not help thinking how the old days and the old ways were gone forever.

It was a relief to get back to Apia in October, and

begin the actual work of making the new home, while Lloyd went off to England to pack up their furniture. During their absence some work had been done. Six or eight acres of land had been cleared and a rough cottage built there. The path down to Apia had been marked a little clearer. Pigs and ducks, horses and cattle, were housed in makeshift places. Otherwise, everything must still be done.

How furiously Louis and Fanny worked during the next few months, with five or six native boys to help them. Building pigpens, rubbing down overworked horses, planting corn and onions and lettuce, clearing the road so that they could get back and forth to town more easily. For hours at a time Louis was alone in the forest, hacking away with a wood-knife, while the strange island birds sobbed like children, or barked like dogs, as he said, around him. He also bought for himself a small horse, Jack, which he rode proudly back and forth to town with a pair of spurred riding-boots on his feet. These boots were his dearest possession. He now boasted that he would "die in his boots" when his time came, instead of "dying in a ditch," as he had said long ago in France.

Nor was the outdoor work all. For hours each day he pored over his writing, turning the thick note-book of facts into a series of travel letters for Mr. McClure's

newspaper in America. These letters were not the great
book about the South Seas he meant to write some day.
But how could he write a great book, when Fanny insisted that he should do no such thing? How her brown
eyes flashed when she told him that he should write
South Sea stories, not a mere book of facts. Perhaps she
was right, but it upset him to quarrel with her.

During those months, too, he was learning the
Samoan language, so that he could feel more at home in
his new country. How like him that was. And sometimes
he wrote poems, something he did no matter where he
was or what he was doing. All his life he had written
poems when the poetic mood was on him.

One of these poems, written in the South Seas, described his wife. It said,

> "Trusty, dusky, vivid, true,
>   With eyes of gold and bramble-dew,
>   Steel-true and blade-straight,
>   The great artificer
>   Made my mate.

> Honour, anger, valour, fire;
>   A love that life could never tire,
>   Death quench or evil stir,
>   The mighty master
>   Gave to her.

Teacher, tender, comrade, wife,
A fellow-farer true through life,
  Heart-whole and soul-free
The august father
  Gave to me."

After Christmas he was more often in the house, with
the rain drumming on the iron roof, for the rainy season
had come. In the tropics they do not have summer and
winter, they have a dry season from April to November,
and a wet season from November to April. While the
wet season was still on, he sailed away to Australia to
meet his mother and get the mail from England. Already
he knew what a thrill the monthly mail-bag could give
him.

The mail itself brought a disappointment. Some of his
travel letters had been printed, and Colvin did not like
them. Were they really good or bad? It was hard to tell.
However they were, he must continue to write them, in
order to pay for the new home on the mountainside. A
new house was being built for him in the center of the
cleared land, looking out over the sea. Soon Lloyd would
be back from England; his sister, Mrs. Strong, was coming from Honolulu with her son, Austin. With his
mother and Fanny and himself there would be six in the
family.

Hiding his disappointment over the letters, he worked

hard on the new home, which he hoped to make a sort of paying farm. By April, the house was finished and the grounds laid out. The name of the estate was Vailima, which meant, in Samoan, Five Streams, for there were five streams flowing down the mountain through his land. The house itself stood in a grove of cocoanut trees, surrounded by a hedge of bright red hibiscus flowers. Above it waved the English flag.

Down below the house was a paddock for the horses and cows. On one side was the garden, already planted with bananas, lemons, pineapple, sweet potatoes, pumpkins, lettuce and onions, and breadfruit. This garden was Fanny's special pride. How enthusiastically she worked in it. But Fanny worked enthusiastically at everything.

In June Lloyd came, and with him crates and boxes of furniture. The books must all be varnished so that their covers would not mildew. How happy Louis was setting out his books of Scottish history in the painted bookshelves in his room. Rifles and native weapons hung there, too, mostly for ornament, although the Samoan Islands were not entirely peaceful at that time. Often, during the next three years, he fretted over the way the islands were governed by the white men.

Good servants for the new home were not easy to find. Outside there was a native overseer in charge of a gardener, a cattle boy, and three or four other boys. Inside there were more boys and Talola, the cook, dressed in a short white kilt, with a red flower behind his ear. This lava-lava, or white kilt, was all the clothing the natives wore in warm weather. How strange they looked, barefoot and brown, padding noiselessly around the house.

Every morning before six, one of these native boys brought Louis his breakfast in his room. After breakfast he wrote until nearly eleven o'clock. Lunch came at eleven, downstairs in the dining room with the family. After lunch, he worked, or weeded the garden, or rode down into Apia on business. Dinner came at five; afterward they all played cards or chatted with visitors. By eight o'clock Louis was alone in his room, reading and nibbling a cracker. Before ten o'clock he was sound asleep for the night.

By October he had finished his travel letters, later published as a book called *In the South Seas*. He had also written another South Sea story, called *The Beach of Falesa,* and had finished *The Wrecker* with Lloyd. Now he was busy writing a book about the Samoan Islands, called *A Footnote to History.* The natives in the islands called him Tusitala, which meant the story-teller. During that year and the next, Louis made a great deal of money from his writing.

January came, and he was planning a novel about a woman on a tropical plantation. By now he realized that his own plantation would never be a paying farm. Too many other white men in the islands paid their men starvation wages. Louis was generous and kind. He could not bear to underpay his men in order to make money on his pigs and pineapples. So he put away that idea, and turned to his writing.

If only the South Sea material would go more easily into books. Why it would not, he was never quite able to say. But the fact was, it wouldn't. The next book he wrote was a Scottish novel, a sequel to *Kidnapped,* called *David Balfour.* Far out in the South Seas, this exiled author wrote about Edinburgh and the Scottish moors. The book was wholly successful. He was now forty-one years old.

Chapter XXXII

Fair the day shine as it shone on my childhood—
Fair shine the day on the house with open door;
Birds come and cry there and twitter in the chimney—
But I go forever and come again no more.

DURING THE LAST days of 1892, and most of 1893, there came a change in Louis' feelings. For some reason he could scarcely write at all. This filled him with fear, for carpenters were already at work building an expensive new addition to his house. The whole downstairs of this new addition was to be a great dining hall, fifty feet long, and lined with imported redwood from California. An elaborate house, a family of six or seven people, a dozen servants, the whole of a tropical plantation depended on Louis' being able to write.

No wonder "the thin man," as the natives sometimes called him, often looked tired and anxious. Alone in his bedroom, where he also did his work, he struggled to make a fresh start. Lloyd's sister, Mrs. Strong, now took

195

dictation from him, for pain and stiffness in his hand, called writer's cramp, made it hard for him to use a pen. Secretly he longed for his "ain gray town" of Edinburgh, the "hills of home" as he called them in a poem.

In this state of mind, he began a new book about Scotland, the story of a French prisoner in Edinburgh Castle in the year 1813. This book was called *St. Ives*. It told a charming story, but did not come easily. At times he laid it aside to work on a history of his father's family, to be called *A Family of Engineers*. With Lloyd, too, he was writing a South Sea book, *The Ebb-Tide*.

The natives, who had come to love Louis, saw this change in their master, and were full of sympathy for him. Perhaps they, more than his family, who were used to his wonderful courage and brightness, felt that something was wrong with him. Louis himself struggled to hide his growing feeling of strain.

The year wore on, and there was political trouble in Samoa. England, France, and the United States, each of whom shared in the government of the islands, did not run things smoothly. The native chiefs and warriors rose up in rebellion. Louis felt that they deserved good treatment, and would be quieter if they got it. Many times he tried to make this clear in his letters to people back home.

In October he went away to Honolulu for a rest, and instead became ill and feverish there. Brought back home, he was ill again in January. Sosima, his valet as well as the house butler, grieved to see him so low-spirited. How faithfully he waited on his master, doing what Louis wished before he even asked for it. Louis now had a new bedroom in the new house, a room which was really a walled-in section of the upstairs porch, with one window looking out to sea, the other up at the wooded mountain, called Vaea, at the side of the house. Long ago Louis had said that when he died he wished to be buried on the top of Mount Vaea.

When summer came he felt better. He grew more cheerful, and was able to work more steadily. The book about the French prisoner, whose name was St. Ives, came out of the drawer and began to flow on to the paper. By September he had written most of this charming story. In September, too, he began a new Scotch novel, called *Weir of Hermiston,* a fine, meaty book. What pleasure it gave him to be writing once more in the solid fashion of a successful author.

November thirteenth, his forty-fourth birthday, he gave a party for his native friends. One hundred Samoan men and women came, bringing amazing presents. Live turtles, fans, live pigs tied to poles, mats made from the softest grass that grew in the islands. In return, Louis and his family served a royal banquet. Pigs roasted, pigs baked, salt beef and pork, eight hundred pineapples from Lloyd's garden, bananas, sugar cane. There were tin boxes of crackers, too, and canned salmon, because the natives loved these rare European delicacies, as they thought them.

Poems were read. There was dancing. No one doubted that Tusitala would be with them many more birthdays.

The truth, however, was very different, and very tragic. On the night of December third, less than a month after the birthday party, Robert Louis Stevenson died suddenly during the evening.

All the last day he showed no particular signs of illness. In fact, he worked steadily at *Weir of Hermiston,* now two-thirds finished. In the late afternoon he came down to find Fanny gloomy and troubled. Together they played a game of cards, before preparing an early supper. Fanny on the porch was mixing salad. Louis, coming back from the storeroom, suddenly stopped and put his hands up to his head.

"What was that?" he asked, as if he had felt a sudden sharp stab of pain.

In a moment he was kneeling on the floor, and that was all the suffering he knew, for almost immediately he lost consciousness. Calling someone to help her, Fanny carried him into the house. Doctors came. A cot was brought down to the great hall. But Louis, poor tired Robert Louis Stevenson, was in a sort of sleep. About eight o'clock he drew his last breath, lying there on the cot with his boots on the floor beside him.

Chapter XXXIII

So, as in darkness, from the magic lamp,
The momentary pictures gleam and fade.

IT WAS HARD for Louis' family and friends to realize that
he was gone, although no one doubted that he was glad
to rest. The fight for health and strength had been a bitter
one. Good work lay behind him. What everyone wished
now was to give him the kind of burial he would have
liked.

The first task was to cut a path to the top of Mount
Vaea, overlooking the sea. All the next morning a
band of two hundred natives worked willingly on the
mountainside, cutting their way gradually upward with
wood-knives and axes. In the hushed house down below
them, many things had to be done. Louis lay in the great
hall with the British flag spread over him. The room was
a mass of bright flowers. All morning a stream of Samoan
friends came bringing these flowers, and the soft, sweet-

smelling grass mats that were their dearest possessions.

In the afternoon the party formed to climb the mountain. It took forty strong men, working in relays, to carry the sleeping Tusitala up to the top. There on a narrow, flat ledge, no bigger than a room, his grave had been dug. There, as evening fell, and the stars came out, he lay quietly resting.

As soon as it could be arranged, a tombstone was placed over his grave. On one side it said in Samoan, "The Tomb of Tusitala." On the other side, in English, were his own words:

> "Under the wide and starry sky,
> Dig the grave and let me die.
> Glad did I live and gladly die,
> And I laid me down with a will.
>
> This be the verse you grave for me;
> *Here he lies where he longed to be;*
> *Home is the sailor, home from the sea,*
> *And the hunter home from the hill.*"

Robert Louis Stevenson, the treasure hunter, was at rest.

Bibliography

Robert Louis Stevenson's Works

"Complete Works," with prefaces by Mrs. Stevenson.
   Biographical Edition 30 vol. New York: Charles Scribner's Sons,
      1907-1912.
         Treasure Island.
         Prince Otto.
         Kidnapped.
         The Black Arrow.
         The Master of Ballantrae.
         The Wrong Box, in collaboration with Lloyd Osbourne.
         The Wrecker, in collaboration with Lloyd Osbourne.
         David Balfour.
         The Ebb-Tide, in collaboration with Lloyd Osbourne.
         *Weir of Hermiston; The Misadventures of John Nicholson;
            The Story of a Lie; The Body-Snatcher.*
         St. Ives.
         New Arabian Nights.
         More New Arabian Nights; The Dynamiter, in collaboration
            with Mrs. Stevenson.
         The Merry Men and other tales and fables; *Dr. Jekyll and
            Mr. Hyde.*
         An Inland Voyage.

Island Nights Entertainments.

Travels With a Donkey.

Virginibus Puerisque and other papers.

Familiar Studies of Men and Books.

The Amateur Emigrant; The Silverado Squatters.

Memories and Portraits.

In the South Seas.

Across the Plains with other memories and essays.

Essays of Travel and *In the Art of Writing.*

Lay Morals and other papers.

Complete Poems: A Child's Garden of Verses, Underwoods. Ballads.

Letters, edited, with an introduction, by Sidney Colvin.

"The Best Thing in Edinburgh," an address by Stevenson to the Speculative Society of Edinburgh, March, 1873. San Francisco, John Howell, 1923.

"Memoirs of Himself," an unfinished autobiography presented by Stevenson to his amanuensis and later sold to H. E. Widener. *Cornhill Booklet,* pp. 55-68. Boston, 1914.

"New Letters of Robert Louis Stevenson" (to Lady Colvin), with introduction and notes by Sidney Colvin. *Empire Review:* Vol. 37, pp. 559-573; Vol. 38, pp. 699-712; 821-833. London, 1923.

"Poems by Robert Louis Stevenson," hitherto unpublished, with an introduction and notes by George S. Hellman. Boston: The Bibliophile Society. Printed for Members only, 1916.

Also Consulted

"The Works of Robert Louis Stevenson," edited by Sidney Colvin. Edinburgh Edition, 28 vol. Edinburgh: T. and A. Constable, 1894-1898.

First Editions of

An Inland Voyage. London: C. Kegan Paul, 1878.

Travels With a Donkey. London: C. Kegan Paul, 1879.

Treasure Island. London: Cassell and Co., 1883.

A Child's Garden of Verses. London: Longman's Green, 1885.

Kidnapped. London: Cassell and Co., 1886.

The Black Arrow. London: Cassell and Co., 1888.

The Master of Ballantrae. London: Cassell and Co., 1889.

Catriona. London: Cassell and Co., 1893.

Works About Robert Louis Stevenson

—— "A Catalogue of the Stevenson Collection in the Library of H. E. Widener," with a memoir by A. S. W. Rosenbach. Philadelphia: Privately Printed, 1913.

—— "First Editions of the Works of Robert Louis Stevenson with Other Stevensoniana," exhibited at the Grolier Club No. 5-28, 1914. New York: The Grolier Club, 1915.

—— *Robert Louis Stevenson Memories,* a book of pictures. London: Peter Davies, Ltd., 1912.

Anderson, A. M. "David Balfour, Yr., of Shaws, Advocate," *Juridical Review,* Vol. 33, pp. 245-269. Edinburgh, 1921.

Baildon, A. B. *Robert Louis Stevenson: A Life-Study in Criticism.* New York: A. Wessels Co., 1901.

Balfour, Graham. *The Life of Robert Louis Stevenson.* New York: Charles Scribner's Sons, 1912.

Barrie, Sir J. M. "R. L. S." *An Edinburgh Eleven: Pencil Portraits from College Life.* New York: Lovell, Coryell and Co.

Benson, E. F. "The Myth of Robert Louis Stevenson." *The London Mercury,* Vol. 12, pp. 268-283, 372-384. London, 1925.

Black, Margaret Moyes. *Robert Louis Stevenson.* Edinburgh and London: Oliphant Anderson and Ferrier, 1898.

Bland, Henry Meade. *Stevenson's California.* San Jose, California: The Pacific Short Story Club, 1924.

Bridges, Robert. *Robert Louis Stevenson.* Warner's Library of the World's Best Literature, Vol. 24, pp. 13927-13936.

Brown, George Edward. *A Book of Robert Louis Stevenson: Works, Travels, Friends and Commentators.* London: Methuen and Co., 1919.

Carre, Jean Marie. *The Frail Warrior,* translated by Eleanor Hard. New York: Coward-McCann, 1930.

Cather, Katherine Dunlop. "Robert Louis Stevenson." *Younger Days of Famous Writers*. New York: The Century Co., 1925.

Chalmers, Stephen. *The Penny Piper of Saranac*, with preface by Lord Guthrie. Boston: Houghton Mifflin Co., 1916.

Chesterton, G. K. *Robert Louis Stevenson*. London: Hodder and Stoughton, 1927.

Clarke, W. E. "Robert Louis Stevenson in Samoa." *Yale Review*, Vol. 10, pp. 275-296. New Haven, 1921.

Colvin, Sidney. "Robert Louis Stevenson," *Dictionary of National Biography*. Vol. 18, pp. 1132-1142. Oxford, 1921.

Colvin, Sidney, Edmund Gosse, and others. *Robert Louis Stevenson, His Work and His Personality*. London: Hodder and Stoughton, 1924.

Cornford, Leslie Cope. *Robert Louis Stevenson*. Edinburgh: W. Blackwood and Son, 1899.

Cunningham, Alison. *Cummy's Diary*, a diary kept by Robert Louis Stevenson's nurse, while traveling with him on the continent in 1863. London: Chatto and Windus, 1926.

Dark, Sidney. *Robert Louis Stevenson*. London: Hodder and Stoughton, 1931.

Douglas, George Brisbane Scott (editor). *A Cadger's Creel: the Book of the Robert Louis Stevenson Club Bazaar*. Edinburgh: W. Brown, 1925.

Douglas, R. B. "Stevenson at Fontainebleau." *MacMillan's Magazine*, Vol. 1 New Series, pp. 340-348. New York, 1906.

Eaton, Charlotte. *A Last Memory of Robert Louis Stevenson*. New York: Thomas Y. Crowell Co., 1916.

Ferguson, A. S. "Stevenson the Dreamer." *Queens Quarterly*. Vol. 30, pp. 26-36. Kingston, Canada, 1922.

Field, Isobel. *Robert Louis Stevenson*. Saranac Lake, New York: Stevenson Society of America, 1920.

Franklin, Viola Pierce. *Stevenson in Monterey*. Salem, Oregon: Statesman Publishing Co., 1925.

Gosse, Edmund. "Personal Memories of Stevenson." *Century*, Vol. 28, pp. 447-455. New York, 1895.

Guthrie, Charles John. *Robert Louis Stevenson: Some Personal Recollections.* Edinburgh: W. Green and Son, 1920.

Hammerton, John A. *Stevensoniana: An Anecdotal Life and Appreciation of Robert Louis Stevenson.* Edinburgh: J. Grant, 1910.

Hamilton, Clayton. *On the Trail of Stevenson.* New York: Doubleday Page and Co., 1915.

Hellman, George S. "The Stevenson Myth." *Century,* Vol. 105, pp. 240-253. New York, 1922.

—— *The True Stevenson: A Study in Clarification.* Boston: Little Brown and Co., 1925.

—— "Stevenson's Annotated Set of Wordsworth," *The Colophon,* Part 7. New York, 1931.

Lisle, George. "Robert Louis Stevenson and Some Savages on an Island." *Cornhill Magazine,* Vol. 51, pp. 706-712. London, 1921.

Low, Will H. *A Chronicle of Friendships.* New York: Charles Scribner's Sons, 1908.

Lucas, E. V. *The Colvins and Their Friends.* London: Methuen and Co., 1928.

Macdougall, Margaret Armour. *The Home and Early Haunts of Robert Louis Stevenson.* Edinburgh: W. H. White and Co., 1895.

Masson, Rosaline Orme. *The Life of Robert Louis Stevenson.* New York: F. A. Stokes Co., 1923.

North, Ernest Dressell. "A Bibliography of Robert Louis Stevenson." *The Bookman,* Vol. 4, No. 1, pp. 81-85. New York, 1896.

Osbourne, Katharine D. *Robert Louis Stevenson in California.* Chicago: A. C. McClurg and Co., 1911.

Osbourne, Lloyd. *An Intimate Portrait of Robert Louis Stevenson.* New York: Charles Scribner's Sons, 1927.

—— "Stevenson at Play." *Scribner's Magazine.* Vol. 24, pp. 709-720. New York, 1890.

Overton, Jacqueline M. *The Life of Robert Louis Stevenson for Boys and Girls.* New York: Charles Scribner's Sons, 1930.

Rivenburgh, Eleanor. "Stevenson in Hawaii," with illustrations. *The Bookman,* Vol. 46, pp. 113-124, 294-307, 452-461. New York, 1917-1918.

Saint-Gaudens, Augustus. "Stevenson and Others." *Reminiscences of Augustus Saint-Gaudens,* edited and amplified by Homer Saint-Gaudens, New York: Century Co., 1913.

Shipman, L. E. "Stevenson's First Landing in New York." *Book Buyer,* Vol. 13, pp. 13-16. New York, 1896.

Simpson, Evelyn Blantyre. *Robert Louis Stevenson's Edinburgh Days.* London: Hodder and Stoughton, 1898.

—— *The Robert Louis Stevenson Originals.* New York: Charles Scribner's Sons, 1913.

Steuart, J. A. *Robert Louis Stevenson.* Boston: Little Brown and Co., 1924.

Stevenson, Fanny Van de Grift Osbourne. *The Cruise of the "Janet Nichol" Among the South Sea Islands,* a diary by Mrs. Stevenson. New York: Charles Scribner's Sons, 1914.

Stevenson, Margaret Isabella Balfour. *From Saranac to the Marquesas and Beyond,* letters written by Stevenson's mother during 1887-1888 to her sister. New York: Charles Scribner's Sons, 1903.

—— *Stevenson's Baby Book,* a record of the sayings and doings of Stevenson during his early years, as kept by his mother. San Francisco: Printed by John Howell for J. B. Nash, 1922.

Strong, Mrs. Isobel. *Robert Louis Stevenson.* New York: Charles Scribner's Sons, 1911.

Strong, Mrs. Isobel, and Osbourne, Lloyd. *Memories of Vailima.* New York: Charles Scribner's Sons, 1902.

Swinnerton, Frank A. *Robert Louis Stevenson, A Critical Study.* London: M. Secker, 1914.

Trent, William P. (editor). *Stevenson's Workshop,* with 29 ms. facsimiles. Boston: The Bibliophile Society, 1921.

Watt, Francis. *R. L. S.* New York: Macmillan Co., 1913.

About the Author

ISABEL PROUDFIT is well known in the book field. She has written biographies of Hans Christian Andersen, Robert Louis Stevenson, Mark Twain, Noah Webster, James Fenimore Cooper. She has also written charming stories for young children, some of which have appeared in book form, others in children's magazines. Before turning to juvenile writing, Mrs. Proudfit was a reporter covering important assignments for newspapers in New York City and London. Although her childhood was spent in Illinois, she lived for many years on a farm in Connecticut and now makes her home in New York City.